MW00614313

The GraceLife

What Philippians Teaches Us About Loving One
Another Relentlessly

Joseph Davis

Copyright © 2018 by **Joseph Davis**

All rights reserved. No part of this publication may be reproduced, distributed, or transmitted in any form or by any means, without prior written permission.

Unless otherwise noted, all Scripture quotations are taken from the ESV® Bible (The Holy Bible, English Standard Version®) copyright © 2001 by Crossway, a publishing ministry of Good News Publishers. ESV® Text Edition: 2011. The ESV® text has been reproduced in cooperation with and by permission of Good News Publishers. Unauthorized reproduction of this publication is prohibited. Used by permission. All rights reserved.

Scripture quotations marked (KJV) are taken from the King James Bible. Accessed on Bible Gateway. www.BibleGateway.com.

Scripture quotations marked (NIV) are taken from the Holy Bible, New International Version. Copyright © 1973, 1978, 1984, 2011 by Biblica, Inc.® Used by permission. All rights reserved worldwide.

Scripture quotations marked (NKJV) are taken from the New King James Version®. Copyright © 1982 by Thomas Nelson, Inc. Used by permission. All rights reserved.

Sermon To Book
www.sermontobook.com

The GraceLife / Joseph Davis
ISBN-13: 978-1-945793-53-0
ISBN-10: 1-945793-53-8

This is a book about how to love your church family. With that in mind, I want to start off by thanking all the church families I have been a part of, who strove to love me even when I made it difficult.

From Temple Heights Baptist in Tampa, FL, to Three Rivers Baptist in Columbia, SC, to our extended church family in Sarasota at Covenant Life Presbyterian Church, South Shore Community Church, and Church of the Palms (the Garden congregation—you know who you are!), you all have taught me what it means to live in grace with one another.

I specifically want to thank Pastor Dan Olson and our church family that was in New Hyde Park Baptist Church in New York. At the darkest time in our lives, you loved my wife, Laura, my son, Ben, and me in ways we will never, ever forget. Your compassion, sacrifice, and hugs left a permanent impact on us and have made me a better pastor.

I also thank my current church family at GraceLife Sarasota for their constant love and encouragement. From the moment we launched, we knew God was creating something very different and very special! I love you all.

Thanks also to C.Y. for the rough job of editing my first draft!

Lastly, I want to thank my wife, Laura. Your patience and your sacrifice for ministry have made this book possible.

CONTENTS

Relentless

Relentless love—what a great expression! And what a great way to characterize both God's love toward us and the way He wants us to love each other.

I've known Joe Davis for a number of years now, both up close and across many miles. Joe doesn't just talk about relentless love. That's how he lives. That's how he does ministry. He's planting a church that embraces those values as central to who they are.

And I'm so glad he has taken the step now to write about it to encourage the church here to love that way. He does this sharing openly from his own experiences, with both authenticity and humility.

Joe understands Scripture as transformational and wants to encourage other Christians to see the development of the way they love. Relentlessly.

As you read this, you will gain a sense of his heart for ministry and devotion to the Word. May the Lord use it to expand the way you love God and others, whether you read it alone or in a small group. Look for God to stretch your understanding of love.

—*Pastor Dan Olson*
New Hope Church of Long Island, Westbury, NY

INTRODUCTION

The Amazing GraceLife

In September of 2007, while I was pastoring in a church in New York, my wife and I lost our eighteen-year-old daughter, Sarah, in a car accident a block from our house. Sarah was killed by a woman who was speeding through an intersection. My wife and I were completely broken; without a doubt, this was the most painful experience of our lives. Through the process of grieving, God worked in our hearts and led us to forgive and reach out to the woman who killed our precious daughter. God enabled us to show her grace, just as He had extended His amazing grace to us.

This personal story exemplifies much of what we'll be discussing in this book. Grace is unmerited favor bestowed through the gifts of love and mercy. What God has done for us through His Son, Jesus Christ, is the ultimate example of grace. When we truly grasp this gift, the ability to live in grace with those around us grows supernaturally in our hearts and we, too, can extend grace in ways that defy common sense.

Look at the Apostle Paul, the author of Philippians. Paul, who was initially known by his Hebrew name, Saul, had been fortunate to be born a Roman citizen in a time when people spent huge amounts of money to buy this coveted citizenship. He was also a Pharisee, which meant he was a leader of his fellow Jews. People looked up to him. Saul had it all.

When a new guy appeared on the scene and began building up a following, Saul personally worked to crush the new sect with relish. His name was feared by Christians throughout the Roman Empire. That is, he was feared until, on a country road, in a flash of blinding light, God reversed Saul's path of bitter oppression toward a life of grace. As he transitioned into ministry as "an apostle to the Gentiles" (Romans 11:13), he became known by his Roman name, Paul.

By studying Paul's letter to the Philippians, we will see an incredible example of what I call the "GraceLife" embodied in his relationship with them. The way in which Paul and the members of the church at Philippi related to each other exemplifies a relentless love based on concepts such as shared sufferings, shared victories, and a deep gratitude for each other. Paul's relationship with the Philippians was dynamic, passionate, sacrificial, and full of commitment to one another, no matter the circumstances. They truly lived the GraceLife together, and the same is possible for us in our churches and communities.

For a clearer understanding of the concept of GraceLife in this biblical book, we'll focus on three aspects of the passages we are studying:

1. **The *history* of the particular passage:** Who is the author? What was happening in the author's life at the moment he wrote these words? What was happening with the readers?
2. **The *theology* of that passage:** What does God do? What is God trying to teach us through this section, and what spiritual lesson can we learn from it?
3. **The *devotional* aspect of that passage:** How can we best apply the theology to our lives, and what does God want us to do with the theology that the passage carries?

As you begin this journey through Philippians, open your mind and heart to view the passages through both the historical and the theological lenses. I pray that you will gain a rich blessing from the book of Philippians due to a better understanding of its context. My goal is to highlight how, based on the model of Paul and the members of the church at Philippi, we can love and live together in our churches today, embodying the GraceLife.

A set of reflective questions and an application-oriented action step accompany each main chapter. Please use these questions and action steps as tools to help you process what a life based on God's grace is all about—and begin to live it out for yourself.

CHAPTER ONE

A New Creation

Paul and Timothy, servants of Christ Jesus, to all the saints in Christ Jesus who are at Philippi, with the overseers and deacons: Grace to you and peace from God our Father and the Lord Jesus Christ.

*I thank my God in all my remembrance of you, always in every prayer of mine for you all making my prayer with joy, because of your partnership in the gospel from the first day until now. And I am sure of this, that he who began a good work in you will bring it to completion at the day of Jesus Christ. **It is right for me to feel this way about you all, because I hold you in my heart, for you are all partakers with me of grace**, both in my imprisonment and in the defense and confirmation of the gospel. For God is my witness, how I yearn for you all with the affection of Christ Jesus. And it is my prayer that your love may abound more and more, with knowledge and all discernment, so that you may approve what is excellent, and so be pure and blameless for the day of Christ, filled with the fruit of righteousness that comes through Jesus Christ, to the glory and praise of God.*

—Philippians 1:1–11 *(emphasis added)*

The New Testament book of Philippians is a letter written by the Apostle Paul to the church in Philippi sometime between 60 and 62 AD.[1] The passage selected above illustrates not only how Paul and the Christians at Philippi lived the GraceLife together, but also how we, too, can live the GraceLife.

History: Emotions Running High

According to the traditional scholarly view, Paul wrote the letter to the Philippians during his first imprisonment in Rome for preaching the gospel.[2] Instead of being held in a prison cell, "Paul was allowed to stay by himself, with the soldier who guarded him" (Acts 28:16). Verse 30 of Acts 28 clarifies further that Paul stayed "in his own rented house" (NIV). Even though his living conditions were satisfactory, Paul knew he could potentially be executed. He had appealed to Caesar (Acts 28:19), and a death sentence was a possible outcome of his appeal. It is clear from his tone in this letter that Paul's emotions were running high.

Paul's letter was written to the church at Philippi, an audience made up of Gentile Christians who knew little of the Jewish laws and customs. Despite the long history of animosity between Jews and Gentiles and Paul's own Jewish heritage, his affection for the Philippians ran deep.

The politics and little details of the day no longer mattered as Paul faced the possibility of death. Instead, he measured everything against the benchmark of the gospel. Though he occupied a superior place in society, Paul demonstrated genuine humility toward these Christians whom he loved. While he naturally felt an affinity for the Philippian church, which he founded on his second missionary journey (Acts 16:1–40), Paul's letter to the Philippians reveals a deep love for this group of believers.

This passage in Acts mentions a friend of Paul's named Epaphroditus, a man who delivered a gift from the Philippian church to Paul. Though not specified, the gift most likely was money to support Paul as he traveled around, planting churches. Before his return, Epaphroditus fell so ill that Paul feared he would die. However, Epaphroditus recovered and returned to the church at Philippi with the letter Paul wrote in prison.

This was probably one of the most intense and emotional times in Paul's life. He realized that he might be coming to the end of his days and wanted to make sure that the church in Philippi knew his deep love for them. The book of Philippians is one of the greatest literary explanations of how to express real love for God's people through any situation that might be playing out in your life.

Theology: Grace Transforms Our Relationships

Before his conversion, Paul's mission was to identify and kill Christians. But God saved him. Upon his conversion, this devout Jew and Roman citizen exhibited a miraculous affection and love for these Gentiles in Philippi. Consider for a moment that Paul's favorite people in the world were those whom his heritage had taught him to despise! How did this transformation take place?

The catalyst for this transformation is the foundation for what I call the GraceLife. God's grace transforms our relationships because it transforms us. It is from this point of grace that Paul penned this amazing letter to the Philippians.

Can you imagine what the old Paul would have thought about what his new self was doing? The old Paul would have been shocked and horrified—because he hated Christians, especially Jewish converts to Christianity. The Philippians were Gentile Christians, which made them even further removed from the old Paul's idea of the chosen people.

There are several places in Scripture where Paul referred to the theological concept of the old Paul versus the new Paul. He was speaking from experience when he wrote, "Therefore, if anyone is in Christ, he is a new creation" (2 Corinthians 5:17). The words "new creation" are important. The old life has passed away; the new life has been born. This new life is a gift "from God, who through Christ reconciled us to himself and gave us the ministry of reconciliation" (2 Corinthians 5:18).

Reconciliation, in this case resolving the wrongs between sinners and God, restores people who are without hope when they put their trust in Jesus' death and resurrection. This act of grace brings together transformed people who were at odds and creates vulnerability, intimacy, and sacrifice. Such changes in the way we interact with the people around us are a remarkable and tangible sign that believers are living the GraceLife.

In the passage below, from another New Testament letter, John described how love for each other blossoms when we accept and believe in God's love for us.

> *We know that we have passed out of death into life, because we love the brothers. Whoever does not love abides in death. Everyone who hates his brother is a murderer, and you know that no murderer has eternal life abiding in him.*
>
> *By this we know love, that he laid down his life for us, and we ought to lay down our lives for the brothers. But if anyone has the world's goods and sees his brother in need, yet closes his heart against him, how does God's love abide in him?*
>
> **—1 John 3:14–17**

When God applies His grace to your life, and you become a "new creation" in Him, He transforms your relationships and gives you a supernatural, uncanny ability to love people you don't even know that well.

Just like Paul, once you have experienced the gift of grace from God, you will be able to live the GraceLife, extending it to others.

Affection Born out of Hardship

Other than the bond between family members, grace is the strongest bond that people can have. In fact, grace may be a stronger bond than family, depending on the degree of dysfunction within the particular family. The bond of grace is supernatural because it is forged and founded upon the common ground of the gospel, and it results in a culture of intimacy, vulnerability, and sacrifice. Grace gives individuals freedom to be vulnerable in supernatural ways that surprise and inspire those witnessing such a powerful transformation.

Philippians 1 is a perfect description of relationships forged by grace. Paul was facing the possibility of death, and this personal crisis caused his affection for the Philippians to be deeper, more intimate than he ever could have imagined. The best way I can describe this is by pointing to a dark time in my life, like the one Paul was facing as he wrote this love letter to the Philippians.

In the introduction to this book, I talked about the loss of my daughter in a car accident. I know of no pain greater than losing a child—it is a heartbreaking, gut-wrenching, profound, and paralyzing pain. Our church walked beside us during our profound affliction, and supernaturally, we were able to bask in God's love, expressed through people He had transformed through grace. The comfort and love were overwhelming.

The people's names and faces are forever etched in our memories. Though I don't talk to many of them as much as I used to, on every remembrance of them, I see their faces and am overcome with affection and love for them. Just like Paul said in this first chapter, I think of them and thank God for putting them in our lives. My wife, Laura, and I never could have gone through those dark days without our church family by our side. As I look back over the years, I remember my fellow brothers and sisters with fondness for their spiritual lives, but with a short memory for their weaknesses.

Confidence in God's Grace

You might think that Paul would have been sad at the prospect of never seeing his beloved Philippians again, or that he worried about how well they would manage without him. But Philippians 1:6 explains why Paul looked back with thankfulness and forward with assurance: "...being confident of this very thing, that He who has begun a good work in you will complete it until the day of Jesus Christ" (NKJV).

Paul's confidence was not in the Philippians' ability to continue to be good Christians and make all the right decisions. On the contrary, his confidence was solely in Christ, who saved them and would deliver them to His Heavenly Father (or Heavenly Dad, as I like to call Him), perfect and blameless. Paul knew that the fate of the church in Philippi rested not on his shoulders, but in God's very capable hands.

In verses 9 to 11, Paul further wrote:

And it is my prayer that your love may abound more and more, with knowledge and all discernment, so that you may approve what is excellent, and so be pure and blameless for the day of Christ, filled with the fruit of righteousness that comes through Jesus Christ, to the glory and praise of God.

Devotional: Living the GraceLife

Philippians 1 is a description of how, through God's grace, believers should feel about each other. We're called to live the GraceLife together in a culture of intimacy and

vulnerability and sacrifice. Unfortunately, the busy, fre-
netic nature of our lives often keeps us at arm's length
from each other. A culture of intimacy can't happen without people sharing life together. The reality is that life is
messy. When we live life in close proximity, we annoy
each other, disagree, and step on each other's toes.

But there is good news! Grace sets us free from keeping score. Grace allows us to have a long memory for the
great things God is doing and a short memory for deficiencies in His people.

In verse 7, it becomes clear that Paul held the Philippians in his heart because they partook in his grace, both in
his house arrest and in his ministry. In other words, because the Philippians were living life with him, they
experienced God's gifts through both shared suffering and
shared joy.

Now, I don't know about you, but in my life, I've seen
and experienced some ugly, unloving behavior from
church members. As we spend time together as a church
family, we see through the superficial image that we all
try to project and stare directly at our flawed, imperfect
selves. How do we, in such moments of exposure, avoid
our tendency to keep a long list of wrongs done to us by
those people with whom we share the Christian life?

Let's look to Philippians 1 for advice. Scan verses 9 to
11 and think about the words Paul chose to describe the
relationships that characterized the church in Philippi:
love, knowledge, discernment, excellent, pure, blameless,
and righteousness.

Paul wasn't ignoring the hard things; he was focusing
on the good things. By reading the list above, we can infer

that the church *loved* each other, using *knowledge* and *discernment* to be *excellent, pure, blameless,* and *righteous.* Loving the other people in our church isn't a blind experience, where we ignore or trivialize hurts. Instead, in love, we discern the right time to approach someone and talk about problems. We rely on Jesus to purify us, wipe our own slates clean, and lead us toward righteousness.

In short, we are transformed by Jesus' grace and, as evidence of that grace, share it freely with those around us. Through fellowship and prayer, we live the GraceLife together.

It will be important going forward to recognize that if you truly have received grace, you will have a supernatural desire to live within a culture of vulnerability, a vulnerability that frees your relationships from selfishness, pride, and arrogance. These supernatural relationships founded on grace look and sound just like the one Paul had with this little Gentile church in Philippi.

Chapter One Questions

Question: When has someone from a very different cultural background affected you deeply or profoundly? Why did Paul have a special love for the Philippians, given their very different backgrounds? What effect did this close relationship have on him during his house arrest?

_____

_____

_____

_____

_____

_____

_____

_____

_____

_____

_____

Question: Why is building a culture of vulnerability so difficult for churches? How can you establish one in your church or fellowship? What needs to change before followers of Christ can be truly open with each other?

_____

_____

_____

_____

_____

_____

_____

_____

_____

_____

Action: Think of some of the good things God has done for you and is doing now. Whom has He used to bless you in the past? Take time to pray for those people, and ask Him to show you how you could bring a blessing to others.

Chapter One Notes

_____

_____

_____

_____

_____

_____

_____

_____

_____

_____

_____

_____

_____

_____

_____

_____

_____

_____

_____

_____

_____

_____

CHAPTER TWO

Suffering Together

*I want you to know, brothers, that what has happened to me **has really served to advance the gospel**, so that it has become known throughout the whole imperial guard and to all the rest that my imprisonment is for Christ. And most of the brothers, having become confident in the Lord by my imprisonment, are much more bold to speak the word without fear.*

Some indeed preach Christ from envy and rivalry, but others from good will. The latter do it out of love, knowing that I am put here for the defense of the gospel. The former proclaim Christ out of selfish ambition, not sincerely but thinking to afflict me in my imprisonment. What then? Only that in every way, whether in pretense or in truth, Christ is proclaimed, and in that I rejoice.

*Yes, and I will rejoice, for I know that through your prayers and the help of the Spirit of Jesus Christ this will turn out for my deliverance, as it is my eager expectation and hope that I will not be at all ashamed, but that with full courage now as always Christ will be honored in my body, whether by life or by death. **For to me to live is Christ, and to die is gain.** If I am to live in the flesh, that means fruitful labor for me. Yet which I shall choose I cannot tell. I am hard pressed between the two. My desire is to depart and be with Christ, for that*

is far better. But to remain in the flesh is more necessary on your account. Convinced of this, I know that I will remain and continue with you all, for your progress and joy in the faith, so that in me you may have ample cause to glory in Christ Jesus, because of my coming to you again.
—Philippians 1:12–26 (emphasis added)

History: Paul's Spirituality in His Suffering

Paul was under house arrest in Rome for preaching the gospel. Though he was kept under constant guard (Acts 28:16), he was able to receive guests and freely share the gospel with them (Acts. 28:30–31).

Despite this freedom, however, Paul still experienced suffering. He was no longer able to travel and visit the churches he loved in person to strengthen them and teach them—he couldn't even leave his house. In fact, it seems that he was chained to keep him from leaving (Acts 28:20). Instead of being able to go to those who hadn't heard the gospel, he had to wait for them to come to him. Imagine how frustrating, how heartbreaking it must have been for a gifted teacher and speaker like Paul to be confined to his house when he was used to moving about freely and being personally involved with his beloved churches.

Though he was unable to go to his friends in person, he chose to write this loving letter to the church he founded at Philippi and be present with them through his words. Even in the midst of his suffering, even knowing that he might be facing a death sentence, he was thriving spiritually.

Isn't that amazing? Paul was not just limping along. He

wasn't hopeless and worried like we would expect him to be. Paul's physical reality had no bearing on his spiritual life. He was continuing the work of the gospel even while in chains.

In this passage, he's saying, "I love you so much, I'm willing to be arrested and have this sword of death hanging over my head and suffer separation from you for your benefit." That's soul-stirring love. Grace had caused Paul to undergo a remarkable transformation that altered his entire value system.

Theology: Fellowship Through Suffering

For Michelle, getting saved was a huge turning point in her life. Though she grew up in church, it had always been something she did, not something she believed. In her college years, she experimented with drinking and sleeping around, which left her feeling guilty and ashamed. Thankfully, a friend invited her to church, and Michelle began a new relationship with God that changed everything.

Life was looking good.

But, as you know, life doesn't usually stay "good" forever. Michelle married a Christian man who went into ministry, and she threw herself into reaching out to the women at their church plant. Her husband loved her, and she was making a difference.

Life was good.

There was only one thing missing: a baby. Being a mom was one of the longings of Michelle's heart—and after all, doesn't the Bible promise to meet the longings of our hearts? Month after month went by with no baby. Michelle prayed harder, devoted herself more to her work, and decided that the timing was all wrong and it would happen when God decided it was right.

Life wasn't quite so good anymore.

As months turned to years, Michelle became desperate. She and her husband sought out doctors, who offered solutions that didn't work. The two didn't have money for fertility treatments, and Michelle started to get angry. If she hadn't married a pastor, this wouldn't be a problem. If she'd married someone who could afford fertility treatments, Michelle would be able to get the desires of her heart. Over time, her marriage became a cold, empty place.

Life was bad.

The only one left to blame was God. After all, He could do miracles, couldn't He? He could let Michelle get pregnant easily. Was this a punishment? What kind of God punished His devoted followers this way? Surely He wasn't trustworthy.

Life was really bad.

God Is Always Sovereign

Stepping outside of real, personal, painful suffering and seeing its purpose is difficult, isn't it? While we're watching a loved one lose a battle to cancer, fighting an ongoing battle with depression, or struggling to find work, it can feel impossible to take our eyes off our pain and put them on our Heavenly Dad. Knowing our suffering is for a good purpose doesn't erase the fact that it's painful.

In fact, it is impossible to step outside of your personal pain and suffering and think about others unless you understand the depth of God's sovereignty. Let me show this to you with the imperfect analogy of a parent and a toddler.

If you've ever parented a toddler, you know how hard it can be. Your child sits in his car seat and has a meltdown after you've been driving for an hour. Even though you are only moments away from home, your child doesn't know that. All he knows is that he's tired, he's hungry, and he doesn't want to sit in the car anymore. He kicks, wails, and arches his back, screaming. And all you can do is sigh, knowing that you are almost home.

And what about the tantrums over things that can hurt that child? He's reaching for the knife you put down when the phone rang, and you run over and snatch his hand away. You've saved him real hurt, but all he sees is his unmet desire.

When I think of parents whose children have medical conditions, my heart breaks. There are times when medical procedures are necessary, but painful. Knowing our little one is going to go through something uncomfortable hurts us, too, but we know it's in his or her best interest.

Romans 8:28 tells us, "And we know that for those who love God all things work together for good, for those who are called according to his purpose."

This is God's sovereignty: God working all things together for good.

The concept of God's sovereignty is important to acknowledge if you want your suffering to mean anything. If you want your circumstances, whatever they are, to turn into a blessing, you have to understand that God is in control. Because if you don't think God is in control and it's all just about the choices you make, then your suffering is pointless.

For Michelle, whom we read about earlier in this chapter, her suffering had no point. The ultimate "good" in her eyes was a baby. And, while God walked with her through her sadness and disappointment, His good was not for her to have a baby. We can speculate as to why, but the reality is that we don't know. We may never know. All we can do is choose to trust that God is doing what is best.

The Blessings of Suffering

Paul was able to be joy-filled during his house arrest because he had an understanding of God's sovereignty as he suffered facing execution. Not only was he dealing with fear, frustration, and discomfort with a good attitude, Paul was encouraging others *because of his suffering!*

Here's what's so amazing about God's sovereignty: you will be able to take suffering and turn it into a gift when you trust God.

> And we know that all things work together for good to them that love God, to them who are the called according to his purpose.
> **—Romans 8:28** *KJV*

What the world would look at and call garbage, grace allows us to see as a beautiful blessing to give to others.

The benefits to ourselves are tremendous, too. Nothing

helps us to trust God more than having gone through hard experiences and being able to reflect on God's goodness. His track record for making marvels out of our messes can help us to take the weight of our suffering off our shoulders and put it in His hands with every confidence.

Consider the following ways in which our suffering can be turned into a blessing:

Suffering can inspire others. In verse 14, Paul wrote, "And most of the brothers … are much more bold to speak the word without fear" (Philippians 1:14).

Isn't that amazing? You see, it's easy for us to consider ourselves inspirational when we're successful. But when you suffer, it can inspire others as God brings you through the trial by His sovereign power. Even during suffering, by trusting in our Heavenly Dad, you can encourage someone else to do the same.

Suffering expands your impact. In verse 13, Paul wrote that "it has become known throughout the whole imperial guard … my imprisonment is for Christ" (Philippians 1:13).

Paul's suffering allowed his people to witness throughout the whole palace guard. He was under house arrest for preaching Jesus, and the gospel was spreading like wildfire under the people who arrested him.

Consider my personal story from the introduction about forgiving the woman who killed my daughter. My forgiveness might have been a very personal decision, but its reach has been incredible. Sarah's story is making an impact for God's kingdom that never would have happened without this suffering.

Suffering increases reliance on prayer. Verse 19 says: "...for I know that through your prayers and the help of the Spirit of Jesus Christ this will turn out for my deliverance" (Philippians 1:19).

When you suffer, you learn of your need for Heavenly Dad. And know that, as you suffer, your brothers and sisters who are living the GraceLife with you are praying for you. Their prayers help you carry your burden. Suffering increases our reliance on prayer and makes us humble.

Suffering reshapes priorities. As we walk through seasons of suffering, our priorities are reshaped from selfish to selfless. Paul loved the Philippians so much, he was willing to experience hardship and suffering if it meant the gospel would be furthered and their faith would be strengthened. He said, to paraphrase Philippians 1:12–26, "Look, I want to go home! I'm tired of living this painful life, but you know what? I'll stick around for the benefit of the church."

One day, you're wondering whether you should take the family to Disney World. The next, you may get an urgent phone call that changes everything, and those plans fly out of your mind. What's most important to you changes when you deal with real suffering. What you spend money on and how you spend your time changes as well.

"Consider it pure joy, my brothers and sisters, whenever you face trials of many kinds," we read in James 1:2

(NIV). When I first read this verse, I thought, "Who do you think you are, James? Count it joy when you go through difficult times?" But James goes on, "Because you know that the testing of your faith produces perseverance. Let perseverance finish its work so that you may be mature and complete, not lacking anything" (James 1:3–4 NIV).

When I think of Michelle, from the beginning of this chapter, I can't help but wonder what it would take to change her priorities. What if she learned that the child she was going to have would have a lifelong health condition that would prevent him from ever walking, using the bathroom, or feeding himself? What if she and her husband adopted a child who desperately needed a good home? What if she had complications in her pregnancy that forever changed her life? If she learned that not being able to get pregnant was actually the act of a loving Father who was protecting her, would it be enough to turn her heart back to Him?

Suffering together helps us grow, individually and corporately. If we lived our lives without any difficulties, would we feel a need for God? I know that in my own life, the times when I grew the most and felt closest to Heavenly Dad were when I was crying out to Him for help again and again to get through the day.

In reality, suffering is what produces growth, both individually and corporately. But we don't really like the pain and growth, do we?

Watching my Christian friends suffer has been hard, but their experience is a gift to all of us because they know that God is sovereign, and they trust Heavenly Dad. Suffering is not easy for them, but it's essential. As we watch them grow in their ability to trust God, we experience such joy in His goodness to us.

My wife, Laura, and I suffered terribly when we lost our daughter, Sarah. Some of the most healing times for us were when we shared our grief with others who had been through the same thing. Over the years, we have shared our story with others and it has been a gift to all of us. You see, when we suffer, God calls us to service, to living for the Kingdom in a new and fresh way.

Because of our experience, my wife says that suffering has enabled us to live life in a new way, with one foot in this world and one foot in eternity. This is a perspective similar to Paul's experience described in Philippians.

Paul said, to paraphrase verse 23, "I've got one foot here and I want be with you, I want to help you. But I've got this other foot in eternity. I can't wait to be with Heavenly Dad when the suffering is over."

Devotional: Suffering Together with God's Children

In chapter 1, we discussed the importance of a culture of vulnerability with one another. One of the best ways to be vulnerable is sharing our suffering together. Listening to others, sitting together through grief, and lending a helping hand are all ways that we pass on God's love for us as we live the GraceLife.

Now, this isn't an excuse to talk about every difficult

situation with every Christian we see. That's not suffering together, it's dumping on everyone around us. Normally, our suffering turns our attention inward, on ourselves. Our pain can produce the idea that we are extra special and deserve to be in the spotlight. I'm suffering. Can't you see I'm in pain? Can't you comfort me?

There will definitely be times when a person's suffering will require intense care from the people around him or her. A good sign that you are using your suffering wisely is if you are still caring for others where you can during your suffering.

Perhaps you are dealing with a job loss that is emptying your bank account. Giving money to the couple in your Bible study who are dealing with cancer isn't wise. However, helping that family to do their laundry or visiting in the hospital and watching TV together can make a difference. Perhaps you don't know what to say to the young mother who just lost her husband. However, you can sit with her and listen as she remembers him. Perhaps your life hasn't been touched by divorce and so you are tempted to lecture a struggling young couple about the importance of staying married. Rather, you could offer to watch their children so they can have a night out to work on their marriage.

Amidst your suffering, ask the Lord to help you see His perspective. Pray that you realize you lack nothing when it comes to your spiritual life. You'll come to see your suffering as part of your transformation and a gift to others. The change is miraculous. When you trust God's sovereignty, you can have confidence in the outcome of any situation. Then you experience true joy.

Easy life is, well, easy. But hardship brings generosity. Suffering brings sacrifice, service, and love, then unspeakable joy if you know Jesus and trust His sovereign hand. That's suffering together.

My prayer is that we can see suffering as a gift to our brothers and sisters who are living the GraceLife together with us. Can you imagine how much growth will take place individually if we are vulnerable enough to sacrifice and suffer together corporately?

Chapter Two Questions

Question: How can suffering be a blessing in disguise? Who might have benefited from your past suffering, and why? In what way can your suffering be a gift to others?

_____

_____

_____

_____

_____

_____

_____

_____

_____

_____

_____

Question: How does suffering reshape your priorities? Why is it important for you to recognize God's sovereignty in your trials and struggles? What happens if you fail to acknowledge God's sovereignty?

_____

_____

_____

_____

_____

_____

_____

_____

_____

_____

_____

_____

Action: Think of areas in your life where you are struggling or suffering. Offer them up to God and ask Him to show you His perspective. Pray that this period will be a time of transformation and growth as you trust Him for the outcome.

Chapter Two Notes

_____

_____

_____

_____

_____

_____

_____

_____

_____

_____

_____

_____

_____

_____

_____

_____

_____

_____

_____

_____

_____

_____

_____

Humble Love

So if there is any encouragement in Christ, any comfort from love, any participation in the Spirit, any affection and sympathy, complete my joy by being of the same mind, having the same love, being in full accord and of one mind. Do nothing from selfish ambition or conceit, but in humility count others more significant than yourselves. Let each of you look not only to his own interests, but also to the interests of others. Have this mind among yourselves, which is yours in Christ Jesus, who, though he was in the form of God, did not count equality with God a thing to be grasped, but emptied himself, by taking the form of a servant, being born in the likeness of men. And being found in human form, he humbled himself by becoming obedient to the point of death, even death on a cross. Therefore God has highly exalted him and bestowed on him the name that is above every name, so that at the name of Jesus every knee should bow, in heaven and on earth and under the earth, and every tongue confess that Jesus Christ is Lord, to the glory of God the Father.

—Philippians 2:1–11

One day, Robin, a young woman I know who worked as a substitute teacher in an urban school district, took a job covering for a preschool teacher. As she watched the fathers who dropped off their four-year-olds for the day, she was struck by an interesting observation.

These men were mostly young, no older than in their mid-twenties. Men of this age, Robin knew, were often busy playing video games, partying, or chasing women. In short, they were enjoying being young adults.

The fathers, though they looked like their typical peers, acted completely differently. They entered the room holding their son's or daughter's hand. Patiently, they helped their children take off their backpacks and hang up their coats. Before they left, they knelt down, kissed their children, and said, "I love you, buddy!" You see, once we become parents, we step into a new humility as we serve our precious children.

History: Paul's Authority Through Humility

Paul sets an example in humility for us—"to in humility count others more significant than yourselves" (Philippians 2:3). When we remember that Paul was under house arrest for the sake of the gospel as he wrote this, his words take on a new tone. Because he humbled himself, he could speak with intense authority.

Isn't that opposite of how we think authority works? Paul challenged the Philippians to the same kind of humility first illustrated by Jesus. Even though He was fully God, He made Himself a servant for His creation and even died a shameful death for us. Christ's humble obedience is reflected in Paul's attitude in these verses.

It was through this authentic humility that a great reversal took place. Paul wrote, "Therefore God has highly exalted him and bestowed on him the name that is above every name, so that at the name of Jesus every knee should bow, in heaven and on earth and under the earth, and every tongue confess that Jesus Christ is Lord, to the glory of God the Father" (Philippians 2:9–11).

By first being humble and vulnerable, Jesus accomplished what no one else could. Then, God exalted Him and gave Him the "name that is above every name." Similarly, Paul was beaten and imprisoned for the gospel, yet reached an immeasurable number of people across many generations.

If we choose to do the opposite, to exalt ourselves rather than remaining humble, Matthew 23:12 says we will be humbled anyway: "Whoever exalts himself will be humbled, and whoever humbles himself will be exalted."

Theology: Grace Creates Humility

"Would you rather be the master or the servant?" If asked this question, who among us could honestly answer "servant"?

The position of master brings privilege, comforts, and wealth, along with admiration. Within our human nature is a desire to be served rather than to serve.

Yet, Jesus Himself resisted this human temptation, instead living a life of humility through selfless service in His life and in His death. If anyone ever had the right to sit on a throne and be catered to, it's the God of all creation! Instead, Jesus set an example for us of humble

servanthood throughout the gospels, never once demanding better treatment because He was God. He was so
certain of His identity as the Son of God, He didn't need
people to kowtow to Him.

With that example, it's hard to look at myself and feel
like I'm doing a good job of emulating my Lord. I don't
want to pick up after adults who can do it themselves. I
don't want to take the uncomfortable seat next to the
woman who never stops talking on the long ride to the
airport. Instead, I want to be comfortable and receive my
due accolades, especially whenever I do something humble.

Signs of Arrogance

To understand humility, we first must understand and
call out arrogance. We've all had our arrogant moments,
but have you ever considered that a church can be arrogant, too? An arrogant church might have any of the
following attributes.

Arrogant churches are selfish. Arrogance forces you
to look out for your own needs and interests. Isn't it amazing how, even in church, a place that's supposed to be
dominated by comfort, love, affection, and mercy, we
look out for our own needs and interests through church
programs, through how the money is spent, through the
music, and maybe even the location? Both petty and true,
I've been in churches that fought over such things as the
color of the carpet and what type of coffee pot to buy.

Arrogant churches obsess over politics. Sometimes arrogance is political, moral outrage over people who have a different view. "How can you be a conservative and love Jesus?" "How can you be a liberal and love Jesus?" When this arrogance leads to social correctness, we pick sides and decide that some people are welcome while others are not. And no matter what your ideology, no matter what your political leaning, if you have a church full of arrogance, these things will dominate your obsession.

Oh, how we find such comfort in political outrage. Do you know why? Because it feeds our arrogance and distracts us from our own sinfulness.

Arrogant churches can't love brothers and sisters. Arrogant churches criticize and judge church members. It's hard to love people who are flawed when you can focus on *their* flaws so you don't see your own. Arrogance is a fertile field for criticism.

Arrogant churches crave comfort. An arrogant church has an inward focus, with a culture of comfort for its leadership and congregation. Its members want to feel good about themselves all the time rather than serving others. Within an arrogant church culture, people may use others as means to an end, craving comfort. However, this is certainly not Christlike behavior and its reward, feeling good, isn't real and it isn't lasting. It's a bottomless pit that can never be filled.

Signs of Humility

So, what characteristics do humble people and humble churches have?

Humble churches are welcoming and give comfort. Humble churches are outward focused, serving both the people within the church as well as those in their community. Just as we are drawn to people who do not act like they are better than we are, we are likewise drawn to humble churches where there's no competition and nothing to prove. Humble churches drain away the need to dress a certain way. Different opinions are welcomed and valued.

Humble churches are loving. A lot of very unloving things have been done by the church throughout history. Today, unloving behavior by those who claim to follow Christ is one of the things that is driving away younger members in droves.

Humble love is all about action. Saying nice things isn't enough. People who are humble love those around them by giving of their time, talents, and money. They view God's work as more important than their own comfort and give of themselves accordingly. Humble churches, in the same way, reach out to their hurting members and to the needy in their communities. Love should be the identifiable trait for every church seeking to emulate Christ.

Humble churches are affectionate. There's something humbling about giving a hug, isn't there? You're stepping into someone else's personal space and allowing that person into yours. Those fathers whom Robin watched kneel down and kiss their children were giving up their macho personas to love their children.

Affectionate churches humble themselves by viewing everyone who enters their doors as a human being with a soul. They get to know each other, greet each other warmly, and spend time getting to know what's happening in each other's lives.

Humble churches extend mercy. This is one area in which the church has hurt the gospel throughout history. It's easy to point out someone else's sin and feel superior because we don't struggle with that particular sin. This has become such a problem that there's a movement away from ever discussing sin in some churches for fear of turning people off from the gospel.

However, when people are honest about their own shortcomings, it draws people in. In humble churches, the pastor stands in the pulpit and preaches on a sin problem by sharing his own struggle with it. In Bible study, the members are open about where they struggle, which encourages others to do the same.

When we're honest about our own sin, it's impossible to withhold mercy from others because we see ourselves in their shoes.

Devotional: Living in Humility

In verse 3, Paul said, "Do nothing from selfish ambition or conceit, but in humility count others as more significant than yourselves" (Philippians 2:3). Abandon ambition or accomplishment in your church, at home, or even in your walk with Jesus. What does that mean? It might mean you stop being prideful about how much you read the Bible or how much you pray. It might mean giving up labeling yourself as a prayer warrior or boasting about your position in church. Those are all spiritual conceits and ambitions.

In Matthew 7:1–5, Jesus said:

> *Judge not, that you be not judged. For with the judgment you pronounce you will be judged, and with the measure you use it will be measured to you. Why do you see the speck that is in your brother's eye, but do not notice the log that is in your own eye? Or how can you say to your brother, 'Let me take the speck out of your eye,' when there is the log in your own eye? You hypocrite, first take the log out of your own eye, and then you will see clearly to take the speck out of your brother's eye.*

I call this "depravity amnesia." Have you ever assumed you are above someone in a particular area of maturity? That's arrogance. But isn't that kind of how we work? We look at somebody and say, "I think that you should probably try to do a little better in this area." And if we make these claims without vulnerability and intimacy, our accusations are judgmental.

Philippians 2:3 serves as a reminder not to value ourselves more highly than others. If you understand your own depravity, you will realize that spiritual conceit is a serious matter that is difficult to root out. If there were an app to notify us whenever we fall short, how many times a day would we be reminded not to judge others?

There's no room for spiritual pride at the top in a church. Okay, I'm a pastor. So what? Big deal! I'm also a sinner, and a pretty awful sinner at that, who desperately needs grace every day. I'm not any better than anyone else when it comes to my own struggle with my flesh and my sin. I have the privilege of sharing the gospel at the front of the church, but that privilege doesn't exalt me as a superior person. If your perspective is that you're trying to pull your brother or sister up to where you are, then you aren't loving, you're being critical. Instead, try gently pushing people up. The mindset of "I need to get behind this person and be with them so we go up together" comes from a humble heart.

The next step is to abandon selfish spiritual agendas. In verse 4, Paul said, "Look out not for your own interest but also the interest of others" (Philippians 2:4).

Contrary to popular American thinking, the church does not exist to scratch whatever liturgical itch you may have. It does not exist to meet your intellectual demands or to satisfy your program appetite. God's people do not live to boost your self-esteem or ego in any way. The agenda of the church isn't to satisfy its members.

We get in trouble when we start believing that the church's purpose is to meet our needs. The church's purpose is to achieve God's purpose, and that often happens through our acts of loving, sacrificial service.

For the church to be transformed, individuals must first seek God's heart on humility.

I encourage you to pray and ask God to transform you with a desire to humbly offer others comfort, fellowship, affection, and mercy. Ask Jesus to teach you to become humble as He is humble, to consider others better than yourself, and to seek to be more like Him.

Chapter Three Questions

Question: Both Jesus and Paul demonstrated their authority through authentic humility. How can you show the same attitude? To remain truly humble, what must you recognize and remember about yourself?

_____

_____

_____

_____

_____

_____

_____

_____

_____

_____

Question: What are the signs of an arrogant church? What spiritual conceits and agendas should you watch out for? How can you minister to others instead with the gifts of comfort, love, and mercy?

_____

_____

_____

_____

_____

_____

_____

_____

_____

_____

_____

Action: Set aside some time to examine your attitude toward your brothers and sisters in Christ. Do you truly consider others better than yourself, or do you suffer from "depravity amnesia"? Ask God to show you where you lack humility and to replace your arrogance with His transforming grace.

Chapter Three Notes

_____

_____

_____

_____

_____

_____

_____

_____

_____

_____

_____

_____

_____

_____

_____

_____

_____

_____

_____

_____

_____

_____

_____

_____

_____

CHAPTER FOUR

Relentless Affection

Therefore, my beloved, as you have always obeyed, so now, not only as in my presence but much more in my absence, work out your own salvation with fear and trembling, for it is God who works in you, both to will and to work for his good pleasure.

Do all things without grumbling or disputing, that you may be blameless and innocent, children of God without blemish in the midst of a crooked and twisted generation, among whom you shine as lights in the world, holding fast to the word of life, so that in the day of Christ I may be proud that I did not run in vain or labor in vain. Even if I am to be poured out as a drink offering upon the sacrificial offering of your faith, I am glad and rejoice with you all. Likewise you also should be glad and rejoice with me.

—Philippians 2:12–18

I know why patience and faithfulness are among the fruit of the Spirit: they don't come easily for most of us. We quickly get tired of dealing with the same problems. Annoyance and frustration come more naturally.

We sigh when we ask our children for *the thousandth*

time to pick up their clothes and put them away. When our spouses do that same annoying thing, our tempers rise. The boss is harping on us about filling out the report *again*. And when it comes to slow drivers? Forget it—instant frustration.

Not surprisingly, patience is sparse even in our churches. We lack patience with many we consider our church family. From their struggles, to the style of worship, to the sermon topics, we seem to leave very little room for patience with one another when our personal agenda for the church is being derailed.

We desperately need the help of the Holy Spirit to develop the skills to love each other relentlessly.

History: Paul's Relentless Love for the Philippians

The Philippian church had a record of faithfulness and relentless love. In this letter, Paul was preparing them for the day they would have to stand on their own. He knew that his decision to appeal to Caesar could result in his execution, and he was trying to make sure that no matter what happened, they would be ready to continue without him.

In many ways, the Philippian church was the crown of Paul's Gentile ministry. He had relentless affection for the Philippians, and his excitement for them seemed stronger than for almost any other church. In his letter to them, Paul mentioned the church's faithfulness, sacrifice, affection, and commitment to each other and to the gospel. Philippi had become a model of what Paul wanted the church as a whole to look like.

The Philippians also had a track record of obedience, whether Paul was there or somewhere else (verse 12). As he planted other churches, they remained a steadfast source of love, financial support, and prayer for him.

Paul had faced immense persecution from Jewish people who hated the fact that he was preaching the gospel of Jesus Christ. When he explained that the temple was no longer needed as a place of sacrifice so that people could be connected to God despite their sin, they wanted to kill him for such blasphemy. Through all of this, the Philippians stuck with him.

And when he was facing the possibility of execution at the hands of the Roman government, what did Paul do? He encouraged the Philippians. He had already sacrificed much for the church, but rather than spending his house arrest in anger and bitterness, he was willing to do even more.

Being willing to be "poured out as a drink offering" (Philippians 2:17) is a picture of being completely spent for the benefit of someone else's walk with Jesus. This is the kind of relentless affection Paul had for his churches, and the kind of love God has for you.

How many of us are willing to go that far for another person? Are we willing to relentlessly go to the end, to sacrifice it all so that we, and others, might be closer to Jesus?

Theology: Relentless Affection Is Supernatural

The word *relentless* means "showing or promising no

abatement of severity, intensity, strength, or pace."[3] In other words, one who is relentless is like the unceasing tides of the ocean.

Both the Philippian church and Paul were relentless in their affection for one another. This relentless nature came from the hand of God, whose very character is relentless.

Relentless affection is not derived from our own willpower. Nor is it derived from attending a big conference, listening to Christian music, reading all the Christian bestsellers, going to church every week, or anything else that we venerate in today's modern church. Relentless affection for your church family is a result of the gift of faith.

Paul said, "Not only as in my presence but much more in my absence, work out your own salvation with fear and trembling, for it is God who works in you, both to will and to work for his good pleasure" (Philippians 2:12–13). God's love, which never wavers in intensity, strength, or pace, is alive and at work in you. Take courage and comfort in that thought.

Paul taught many times that relentlessness is a key indicator of whether you can say you are a Christian. Let's look at three examples.

In Galatians 6:9, Paul declared, "And let us not grow weary of doing good, for in due season we will reap, if we do not give up."

Paul also exhorted believers to be "strengthened with all power, according to his glorious might, for all endurance and patience with joy" in Colossians 1:11.

Finally, Paul encouraged believers in Romans 15:5–6: "May the God of endurance and encouragement grant you to live in such harmony with one another, in accord with

Christ Jesus, that together you may with one voice glorify the God and Father of our Lord Jesus Christ."

The Opposite of Relentless Love

What does relentless love look like in our lives? Let me explain by showing you the opposite.

Americans are obsessed with retirement. Now, I'm not talking about stepping away from your job, I'm talking about quitting life. It's the idea of simply stopping all our commitments and doing only the things that we want to do. That's what we talk about all the time, isn't it? "Gosh, I'm so tired of being busy all the time. I can't wait until I'm retired!" Yet for some people, retirement may increase their risk for depression. Perhaps we simply weren't made to quit life.

On the other hand, a man named Steve worked his entire life and was successful in his field of business. He retired a very wealthy man. Most people in his place would start living a leisurely life to reward themselves for all the hard work they had done. Not Steve. He joined the staff at his church and helped the finance department to be smarter about how the church's money was spent. He joined a Life Group with his wife and encouraged the younger couples there. He regularly met with his old business associates to have lunch and to continue discipling them. Steve was relentless in his love and affection for God's people.

When God works in you, let Him have His way with confidence and with great endurance, no matter what your age or your emotional state. As Paul said, "It is God who works in you, both to will and to work for his good pleasure" (Philippians 2:13).

The Fruits of Relentless Love

These are the fruits of relentless love:

Relentless motivation. Paul directed believers to "work out your own salvation with fear and trembling" (Philippians 2:12). This doesn't mean you have to earn your salvation. Salvation is by grace through faith (Ephesians 2:8–10). By studying and working relentlessly, you show evidence that your faith is real, from Heavenly Dad and not from religion.

We don't want good Presbyterians. We don't want good Baptists. We don't want good Catholics. God doesn't need "good" Christians who follow the rules as they go about their busy lives. He wants sinners who have been saved by grace and are relentless in their motivation to bring God's kingdom to those around them. Faith is made evident by this relentless motivation.

Relentless confidence. When people are relentlessly motivated, they will naturally possess relentless confidence. They don't rely on themselves anymore; they are relying on the unfailing God. There's no question of whether they are valuable or capable because Jesus, who is infinitely valuable and capable, has become their identity.

Relentless commitment. Relentless commitment is

perseverance that requires all our effort to complete the task before us. Sometimes it's tempting not to bother, to skip a few meetings or let standards slide. When we understand what Christ did for us on the cross, we are compelled to pursue excellence in completing the job. It is not an option to cut corners or quit before the job is done.

Relentless sacrifice. If you have the gift of faith that gives you relentless motivation, relentless confidence, and relentless commitment, you will relentlessly sacrifice. Those who are committed to Christ willingly sacrifice their time, energy, and finances when God asks. They understand that God gave us everything, and nothing we have is too precious to hold back.

Is my level of sacrifice relentless? Or do I only give when it's convenient—when I can spare the time, money, or talent? Paul urged Christians to be poured out as a drink offering, as a sacrifice in service of each other.

Paul wanted the Philippians to follow his example because he saw the better way: God's way. He desired that they be poured out for each other and for those around them, so that they would be a light to the world. This is what it means to work out your salvation with fear and trembling. Will you allow yourself to be encouraged by the evidence of real faith in your life?

Grumbling and complaining are incongruent with faith and relentless commitment. While selfish protests happen from time to time, consistent attitudes of complaining, griping, and criticizing are impossible when we remember the sacrificial love of Jesus on the cross.

Look at this passage in Hebrews:

> *Therefore, since we are surrounded by so great a cloud of witnesses, let us also lay aside every weight, and sin which clings so closely, and let us run with endurance the race that is set before us...*
>
> **—Hebrews 12:1**

It's hard to be a grumbler when you know He's working in us, and our relentless commitment is for His pleasure.

Devotional: Loving Others Relentlessly

Our love of self often derails us from our affection for each other. When our main concern is ourselves, we become judgmental, unforgiving, and demanding of other people. Sometimes, the sins that derail us are our love for money or possessions. Perhaps our passion for our own agenda is the thing that keeps us from being relentless.

If you find those things constantly prevailing, it may be a sign that your faith is based on what you can do, not on what Jesus did for you. When that happens, we're falling into the trap of religion. Religion is a powerful tool for making us feel that we aren't doing enough to be "good Christians," but it's powerless to make us relentless. Only faith in God's ability can make us relentless in His service. This very faith is itself a gift from God (Ephesians 2:8–9), and living in constant awareness of this fact keeps us in a place of humble adoration. Being aware that we are not saved by our own efforts but by God's grace alone makes our hearts overflow and allows us to respond with relentless gratitude.

Let us set aside the things that keep us from being relentless so that we can embrace relentless love, like Paul had for the Philippians and they had for him.

I pray that God gives us the evidence of our faith manifested in our relentless affection for one another. Without this relentless affection, we are just a group getting together for donuts and coffee on Sunday morning.

The example that Paul and the Philippians set for us demonstrates how we can live our lives poured out in sacrifice and service for each other. It is one of the key ingredients for living the GraceLife.

WORKBOOK

Chapter Four Questions

Question: What does relentless affection look like in practice? Has anyone ever shown you such affection? What effect did it have on you?

_____

_____

_____

_____

_____

_____

_____

_____

_____

_____

_____

Question: Relentless affection is linked to perseverance and commitment. Do you have this kind of commitment to God and to others? Do you have faith, or just religion? How do you know?

_____

_____

_____

_____

_____

_____

_____

_____

_____

_____

_____

Action: Take some time to think about what may be keeping you from demonstrating this degree of affection and commitment. Are you ready to be poured out for the service of others? Ask God to show you where your ego or your own agenda may be keeping you from being one hundred percent committed to Him and His church.

Chapter Four Notes

CHAPTER FIVE

Affectionate Accountability

I hope in the Lord Jesus to send Timothy to you soon, so that I too may be cheered by news of you. For I have no one like him, who will be genuinely concerned for your welfare. For they all seek their own interests, not those of Jesus Christ. But you know Timothy's proven worth, how as a son with a father he has served with me in the gospel. I hope therefore to send him just as soon as I see how it will go with me, and I trust in the Lord that shortly I myself will come also.

I have thought it necessary to send to you Epaphroditus my brother and fellow worker and fellow soldier, and your messenger and minister to my need, for he has been longing for you all and has been distressed because you heard that he was ill. Indeed he was ill, near to death. But God had mercy on him, and not only on him but on me also, lest I should have sorrow upon sorrow. I am the more eager to send him, therefore, that you may rejoice at seeing him again, and that I may be less anxious. So receive him in the Lord with all joy, and honor such men, for he nearly died for the work of Christ, risking his life to complete what was lacking in your service to me.

—Philippians 2:19–30

There are many kinds of managerial styles in the world today. If you've been working long, you've likely had a variety of bosses who like to do things different ways. Some motivate their workers through criticism and fear. Others are quick to drop by for a friendly chat but slow to handle problems.

In fact, affection and accountability seem like they don't usually go together when it comes to our jobs. Bosses might be good at one or the other, but it's rare that they are good at both. However, if you've ever had the privilege to work with a supervisor who holds people accountable and is still affectionate, you know what a great work environment is produced.

Biblical accountability is affectionate. Jesus set the tone for this throughout the Gospels. Time and again, we see Him interacting with people with kindness and devotion without compromising His standards. This powerful passage from Paul shows us how affectionate accountability is a crucial component of the GraceLife.

History: Paul Earned the Right

In this passage, Paul referred to two people, Timothy and Epaphroditus, who helped him in his ministry. Since Paul did not know how long his house arrest would last or if it would end in a death sentence, he planned to send these two talented, qualified men to do a few important jobs.

As we learned in the previous chapter, Paul had relentless affection for the Philippians, and because of this, he was not afraid to tell them when they were wrong. As a man who was charged with their spiritual well-being, he sent some high-caliber accountability to the Philippians.

This move wasn't motivated by a desire to spy on the Philippians; rather, Paul's actions were rooted in love. Paul was concerned about the Philippians and wanted to send Timothy to them, so Paul could be encouraged by good news and relieved from his worries (Philippians 2:19).

Later, Paul wrote that he was going to send Epaphroditus because he wanted to "be less anxious" (Philippians 2:28). In his affection, Paul sent two accountability partners. But these weren't just any two guys; they were specially chosen and assigned to this task.

Theology: Affectionate Accountability

Even though we're called to hold each other accountable, we don't have permission to beat people up with their sin, pointing out every flaw we see. In fact, we need to "earn the right" to get into this intimate part of people's lives.

Paul earned the privilege of holding the Philippians accountable in three ways: credibility, boundaries and targets, and a history of relentless sacrifice.

Credibility

Paul had earned credibility because, as we learned in the previous chapter, he had demonstrated relentless affection, motivation, confidence, commitment, and sacrifice to the Philippian church. Because of his proven reliability, the Philippians could trust who Paul sent in his place.

In Philippians 2:19–22, Paul's words reflect integrity and commitment regarding his special relationship with Timothy. They had ministered together at many different times and in many different places. Both had suffered and celebrated victory together. Many say that Timothy was Paul's closest friend.[4]

Now Paul was under house arrest, and although sending Timothy would likely make Paul's incarceration lonelier and more emotionally challenging, Paul was determined to do it. The Philippians knew Timothy was Paul's right-hand man. They realized that sending him now spoke to how much Paul loved them and how much Paul wanted to make sure that they had accountability.

Why is accountability so important? Because shepherding without accountability is political love that runs only on the surface. Lack of accountability inevitably erodes trust and expectations that we are acting for the good of our community. Accountability, providing it as well as submitting to it, is proof of intimacy and trust. No accountability means there is no relentless affection, no trust, and no real love. It is impossible to live the GraceLife without it.

Boundaries and Targets

Paul carefully set boundaries and targets for accountability that were real and meaningful, not perfunctory in nature. In Philippians 2:23–24, he said, "I hope therefore to send him just as soon as I see how it will go with me, and I trust in the Lord that shortly I myself will come also." Paul then explained the two goals he hoped to achieve by sending accountability.

The Philippian church wasn't a perfect church. There was grumbling going on behind the scenes, to which Paul responded that they should have relentless affection instead of grumbling (Philippians 2:14). Paul sent Timothy and Epaphroditus to deal with the matter.

However, encouragement was equally important to Paul, so he asked to hear all the good things that the Philippians were doing. He wasn't just sending them accountability because they were grumbling; he also wanted to hear about the positive side.

Using Paul's example, we see that accountability needs to have specific, agreed-upon guidelines and purposes ahead of time. Otherwise, resentment will set in, along with distrust and bitterness.

Earning the Privilege

In verses 25 to 27, we read how Epaphroditus nearly died trying to bridge the gap between the Philippians and Paul. Delivering letters, along with communicating ideas and plans, could be dangerous work, and in the process of serving Paul and the Philippians, Epaphroditus almost lost his life.

To paraphrase what Paul said in Philippians 2:9–30, "Epaphroditus was good at making sure he bridged the gap where you were falling short. You have been so faithful because of the things he did to make up for your deficiencies." In short, accountability is a privilege that is earned. However, submitting to that earned accountability is equally important.

Can you see how vicious and sinful it would have been for the Philippians to say, "We don't want to be accountable to him"? But because Epaphroditus had a history of relentless sacrifice, trust, and service, he had earned this privilege. In the same way, if we deny someone with a strong history of service and sacrifice in our lives the privilege of holding us accountable, we are repaying that person's hard work with graceless ingratitude.

Devotional: Practicing Affectionate Accountability

Where faith exists, affectionate accountability also exists. First John 3:14 says, "We know that we have passed out of death into life, because we love the brothers. Whoever does not love abides in death."

Do you understand John? If you do not love your brother or sister, you're living in spiritual death, without a hunger and thirst for Christ and His repentance. In contrast, loving others despite their flaws is evidence that you actually love Jesus.

Affectionate accountability is a natural byproduct of gospel-centered love. It's a key element of the GraceLife. When true love is present in our churches, affectionate accountability is there as well. It is the fertile soil in which we grow and thrive as Christians in intimate, beneficial relationships.

My prayer is that you practice affectionate accountability with the people you love. Earn credibility through relentless love and ensure that your accountability comes with boundaries and targets. Finally, remember that the best way to foster affectionate accountability is by a demonstrated history of sacrifice and love.

What does relentless love look like? It looks like Epaphroditus, who was so relentless in giving of his time, his talent, and his money.

Where does accountability start? From one of the first things we discussed: vulnerability.

Without vulnerability, there will be no accountability. Without accountability, church becomes something you consume rather than something that transforms you. Liturgy and worship will not change you. God's Word and intimate relationships with His people are what change you.

WORKBOOK

Chapter Five Questions

Question: Why must accountability be partnered with affection? Why is accountability important? What could happen to your church if no one were held accountable?

_____

_____

_____

_____

_____

_____

_____

_____

_____

_____

_____

Question: Think of someone in your life who has earned the right to hold you spiritually accountable. What boundaries and targets has he or she set? How has this person established credibility through sacrificial love?

_____

_____

_____

_____

_____

_____

_____

_____

_____

_____

_____

Action: Ask God to show you how to earn the right to practice affectionate accountability with others. Begin to build credibility through acts of relentless love, humility, and sacrifice. Pray for God's grace to transform your heart and your fellowship so that you are abiding in love, not in death.

Chapter Five Notes

_____

_____

_____

_____

_____

_____

_____

_____

_____

_____

_____

_____

_____

_____

_____

_____

_____

_____

_____

_____

_____

CHAPTER SIX

Beware of Dogs

Finally, my brothers, rejoice in the Lord. To write the same things to you is no trouble to me and is safe for you. Look out for the dogs, look out for the evildoers, look out for those who mutilate the flesh. For we are the circumcision, who worship by the Spirit of God and glory in Christ Jesus and put no confidence in the flesh.

—Philippians 3:1–3

There's a path in my neighborhood where I run or walk, depending on how I'm feeling that day. There's a section where a little Chihuahua named Julio forces me to do interval training to get my heart rate up. He's a fast dog, and he's always right on my heels. Picture me running in fear from this tiny, yapping furball.

It's a pretty ridiculous picture, isn't it?

But when Paul talks about dogs in this passage, he's not referring to the canine variety. He's talking about religious people who are just as dedicated to teaching falsehoods as Julio is to protecting his yard. But religious dogs are far deadlier.

History: Paul's Contention with Religious Dogs

At the time Paul was writing to the Philippians, the greatest opposition to the gospel was not the Roman government but Jewish religious leaders.

In Philippians 3, we see a change in tone. In the first two chapters, Paul was warm and affectionate. He loved and cared for the church in Philippi. But there's a shift to righteous indignation and name-calling. The change is understandable. Paul had sacrificed so much to start these Gentile churches, and the church in Philippi was one of his favorites. It's only natural that Paul would be protective of his friends.

But, why such a fierce shift in tone?

Paul had faced a lot of criticism in his ministry. A Jewish man, Paul went to Gentile areas of the Roman Empire that had never heard of Jesus to preach the gospel. Through his actions, God would save the lost, and new churches would start.

In due course, Paul would travel somewhere new and enemies would come behind him and say, "Don't listen to Paul, he's an idiot. He's a heretic. He's an evil man." And they would try to undo all of Paul's hard work. They denied that salvation through Jesus was all a person needed to be connected to Heavenly Dad, or they would take certain parts of the gospel and leave out the rest, twisting Scripture and manipulating teachings for their own ends, often for financial gain.

In fact, Paul said, "Some indeed preach Christ from envy and rivalry, but others from good will" (Philippians 1:15). He also talks about the motives driving people to twist the gospel. Sometimes it was distorted a lot, but that wasn't as dangerous as when it was distorted in subtle ways. You can see why Paul built up a lot of resentment and anger toward these people. He was under house arrest and facing a possible death sentence for preaching the gospel; he was invested. Of course he would be passionate!

Paul knew God's people would face similar persecution, and he warned the Philippian church to prepare for suffering at the hands of the enemies of the gospel.

Not long after Jesus' death and resurrection, the fledgling church experienced what could be described as the first denominational fight: "But some men came down from Judea and were teaching the brothers, 'Unless you are circumcised according to the customs of Moses, you cannot be saved'" (Acts 15:1). In other words, "Yes, you're a Gentile and yes, you're a Christian, but you still have to be circumcised."

Paul and Barnabas and some of the others were appointed to go to Jerusalem to meet with the apostles and the elders regarding the question of whether Gentiles needed to be circumcised. This meeting was called the Jerusalem Council. Luke wrote, "So, being sent on their way by the church, they passed through both Phoenicia and Samaria, describing in detail the conversion of the Gentiles, and brought great joy to all the brothers" (Acts 15:3).

At the Jerusalem Council, Paul and Barnabas declared, "Look what Jesus has done with these people without religion getting in the way. It's just Jesus." Scripture says that they reported what was going on with the Gentiles and the unified decisions brought great joy to all the brothers—in other words, all the Jewish Christians in Jerusalem.

> When they came to Jerusalem, they were welcomed by the church and the apostles and the elders, and they declared all that God had done with them. But some believers who belonged to the party of the Pharisees rose up and said, "It is necessary to circumcise them and to order them to keep the law of Moses"
>
> **—Acts 15:4–5**

Pharisees, who rigidly observed the old ways, were trying to control this spin-off from Judaism by spreading heresy. Everywhere the gospel took root, these evil emissaries were trying to corrupt the Church.

Some argued that Christians needed to follow not only Jesus but also "the law of the temple" (Ezekiel 43:12). "You've got to be circumcised. You must observe the feast days. You've got to dress a certain way, eat certain types of food, and hang out with certain types of people. Jesus isn't enough. You must strive to be religiously perfect and then, with that added to faith, you might make it." But Paul exhorted believers to focus on the good news of Jesus Christ instead of religion.

Theology: Religion Versus the Gospel

The Pharisees had strayed from the path Jesus had set—the path of the gospel. Why was the gospel different and superior to the law?

Author Philip Yancey wrote a book titled *What's So Amazing About Grace?*[5] It includes an anecdote about C.S. Lewis:

> During a British conference on comparative religions, experts from around the world debated what if any belief was unique to the Christian faith. They began eliminating possibilities. Incarnation, well other religions had different versions of incarnation. Resurrection, again other religions had accounts of returning from the dead. The debate went on for some time until C.S. Lewis wandered into the room. What's the rumpus about, he asked and heard in reply that his colleagues were discussing Christianity's unique contribution among world religions. They couldn't figure it out. And Lewis responded, oh that's easy. It's grace. After some discussion, the conferees had to agree. The notion of God's

love coming to us, free of charge, no strings attached seems to go against every instinct of humanity. The Buddhist eight-fold path, the Hindu doctrine of Karma, the Jewish cove-nant, the Muslim code of the law. Each of these offers a way to earn approval from God. Only Christianity dares to make God's love unconditional.

I am inspired when I read that story. It brings tears to my eyes because it is such a simple, yet profound commentary on why the gospel is superior to religion. There is no way to earn salvation, no matter how wonderful a religion may seem. Paul outlined this theology in several passages.

In Romans 3:23, Paul asserted that "all have sinned and fall short of the glory of God." This is you. This is me. You and I don't even come close. And so, we "are justified by his grace as a gift" (Romans 3:24).

And Ephesians 2:8–9 reminds us: "For by grace you have been saved through faith. And this is not your own doing; it is the gift of God, not a result of works, so that no one may boast."

Finally, Hebrews 4:16 says, "Let us then with confidence draw near to the throne of grace, that we may receive mercy and find grace to help in time of need."

Each scripture demonstrates the difference between the gospel and religion. Religion offers ways to become close to God, and personal works ensure the doer will come into salvation. The gospel gives us the truth: we are only saved by grace through faith.

The Apostle John echoed this teaching in John 14:6, declaring the only requirement for salvation: "Jesus said to him, 'I am the way, and the truth, and the life. No one comes to the Father except through me.'" Passage after passage makes this reality clear: only through faith in Jesus is a person saved. Salvation is found in Christ alone.

Religion says: *Obey God's rules and then He will love you.* The gospel says: *God transforms you and enables you to obey.*

Religion says: *God loves good people and He hates bad people.* The gospel says: *All have sinned and fallen short of the glory of God—and He loves them anyway.*

Religion says: *See what I do.*

The gospel says: *Look at what Jesus has done.*

Religious people hide their sin to avoid spiritual embarrassment. Gospel-driven people confess and repent and admit to others that they need help. Vulnerability, creating accountability, becomes a shining light to all. This is the core of what the GraceLife is all about! This is powerful!

There are many opinions about religion and spirituality, but there is only one way to Heavenly Dad: through Jesus, the cross, the resurrection. Throughout the Bible, there's no teaching of Jesus or Paul that states, or even suggests, that all roads ultimately lead to heaven.

Paul warned the Philippians: "Look out for the dogs, look out for the evildoers, look out for those who mutilate the flesh" (Philippians 3:2). His warning to the Philippians extends to believers today.

Consider the following popular examples of false teaching in this generation:

"All roads lead to heaven." If all roads lead to heaven, we're in big trouble because our Jesus is a liar when He says, "I am the way, and the truth, and the life. No one comes to the Father except through me" (John 14:6). If Jesus is a liar, then He's not our Savior.

"Salvation is not secure." In other words, once God saves you it's great, but you could lose your salvation. Scripture says, "No one will snatch them out of my hand" (John 10:28) and "He who began a good work in you will bring it to completion at the day of Jesus Christ" (Philippians 1:6). True salvation always saves. When God saves you, He does a perfect job.

"Jesus did not have to die." Some say Jesus chose death as an object lesson of what true love looks like. He could have saved us without dying, but He thought it would be an exclamation point on His life. But the Bible clearly says otherwise: "For the wages of sin is death" (Romans 6:23), and "without the shedding of blood there is no forgiveness of sins" (Hebrews 9:22). Christ's willing love and sacrifice was the only option.

"The Bible is just traditions, not truth." There are many who claim that the Bible is not ultimate truth but merely an expression of a certain viewpoint based on traditions. This is a particularly popular stance by those who lead what is called the Emergent Church, or something called "Progressive Theology." Certainly, the Bible contains traditions, but Scripture is the inspired Word from God (2 Timothy 3:16).

"Hell isn't real, nor is judgment." It doesn't make

sense to preach mercy from God if there are no consequences for sin. Matthew 25:46 says some will go to eternal punishment, hell, while the righteous, those redeemed by the blood of Christ, go to eternal life.

As pastors and shepherds, it is our crucial responsibility to come up with a way to say these things without being demeaning or discouraging, while also being fair and tough. The reason? These bad theologies rob us of the experience of living the GraceLife because, by taking away the consequences of our sinfulness, we don't need to be transformed.

If we don't need mercy, we don't need the gospel. If we don't need the gospel, we don't need Jesus. And if we don't need to embrace repentance, why change? Why worry about recovery? Why worry about restoration? Why worry about making relationships right if there is no consequence for wrong? Why do we even need each other? Why even have a church? Why anything?

In reality, thanks to Christ, we have everything.

Devotional: Following the Gospel Instead of Religion

Bad theology about the gospel robs us of truly knowing Jesus and the fellowship of His sufferings. We miss out on the joy of Christ and the GraceLife. Life becomes a swirling, sucking eddy of despair, a sea of nominalism, universalism with no real boundary of what is truth and reality and what is just idea and a figment of imagination.

We have no idea where to turn for the rock, the foundation.

Just like little Julio's mission in life appears to be disrupting my morning jog and tearing me limb from limb, bad doctrine will hinder what God is doing in our lives and take the glory away from what Jesus has done for us.

However, love will not let the "dogs" of false religion run wild, because what they teach mutilates our faith.

Followers of Jesus who are in positions of leadership should repeatedly warn people, as Paul warned the Philippians, to be wary of false teachings. They don't offer spiritual healing, fellowship, and most importantly, salvation. This warning should be done in a way that encourages growth, unity, humility, and compassion. The first and best way to identify false teachers would be to answer the following question: Does their teaching try to give man any role in, or credit for, the application of grace? If it does, it's a lie.

Church leaders must be on guard for these things, and, just as Paul did, seek to call out these false teachings boldly and directly. This is vital because false teachings about the gospel and about God's Word will ultimately hinder us from reaping the benefits of the GraceLife, which enables us to live together through the gospel of grace and peace through Jesus.

We don't merely want to provide warnings or win an argument with somebody who doesn't believe that Jesus Christ is the only way to salvation. Fighting helps no one. We don't want to point out false doctrine in a way that makes somebody who doesn't believe in Christ feel like garbage.

But let me be clear: pastoral love will not let the dogs run wild like Julio the Chihuahua does every morning when I run by his yard—because what those dogs teach will mutilate your faith.

Instead, church leaders must constantly correct false beliefs in a way that encourages, strengthens, and equips. We must stay humble and vulnerable and show compassion to those around us who don't yet know that they need unconditional grace and mercy from Jesus. This isn't about winning, it's about building the kingdom of God.

WORKBOOK

Chapter Six Questions

Question: Have you ever been asked how Christianity differs from other major religions? What did you answer? How would you explain God's grace to someone from a non-Christian background?

_____

_____

_____

_____

_____

_____

_____

_____

_____

_____

Question: Why does bad theology prevent us from experiencing all the benefits of the GraceLife? Can false beliefs creep in without you noticing? What kind of things do you find yourself believing instead of relying on God's grace alone?

_____

_____

_____

_____

_____

_____

_____

_____

_____

_____

_____

Action: Think of examples of bad theology you often hear: Jesus did not have to die, all roads lead to heaven, and so on. Write down as many false doctrines as you can. Then, beside each one, plan how you could compassionately refute it in a way that encourages and builds up the hearer.

Chapter Six Notes

CHAPTER SEVEN

Be Really, Really Bad at Religion

*...though I myself have reason for confidence in the flesh
also. If anyone else thinks he has reason for confidence in
the flesh, I have more: circumcised on the eighth day, of the
people of Israel, of the tribe of Benjamin, a Hebrew of Hebrews; as to the law, a Pharisee; as to zeal, a persecutor of
the church; as to righteousness under the law, blameless.
But whatever gain I had, I counted as loss for the sake of
Christ. Indeed, I count everything as loss because of the sur-
passing worth of knowing Christ Jesus my Lord. For his sake
I have suffered the loss of all things and count them as rub-
bish, in order that I may gain Christ and be found in him, not
having a righteousness of my own that comes from the law,
but that which comes through faith in Christ, the righteousness from God that depends on faith—that I may know him
and the power of his resurrection, and may share his sufferings, becoming like him in his death, that by any means
possible I may attain the resurrection from the dead.*
—Philippians 3:4–11

Middle school is one of the worst times of life for many
people. Hundreds of young children going through pu-
berty at the same time are forced to spend seven hours a

day in close proximity to each other. Everyone is testing different identities and experimenting with social rules.

For Emily, middle school was especially frustrating due to her circle of friends. Emily lived overseas and attended an American school that boasted about twenty kids per class, which increased the complexity of peer relationships.

In Emily's class was a girl named Molly who also lived in the same building as Emily's family. Molly was the queen bee of the girls in their class and ruled over everyone with great relish. One day, Emily and Molly were best friends. The next day, Molly would ignore Emily and spread rumors about her.

Emily never knew where she stood with Molly. Even though she followed the "rules" of sixth-grade girls, it was impossible to know whether she was at the top of the pecking order or the bottom until Molly made it clear.

In the same way, the rules of religion are complicated and tricky. If we're able to make up for our sins by doing good, how do we know when we've done enough? What is the conversion rate for sin? Is it one good deed to cancel out one sin? What if I do that good deed but sin while I'm doing it? Do I still get credit for that good deed? Does saying one prayer cancel out my speeding ticket? How do I know if I'm good enough?

History: Paul's Gains Turned to Loss

Let's look at Paul's life before he turned to Jesus.

His impressive credentials are detailed in Philippians 3:5. He said he was "circumcised on the eighth day, of the people of Israel, of the tribe of Benjamin, a Hebrew of Hebrews; as to the law, a Pharisee." In other words, in the social pecking order of Jewish people, he was right near the top. He could say, "Everyone is jealous of my position."

He had been arrogant in his perceived righteousness. In Philippians 3:6, this is how he described himself before his encounter with Christ: "...as to zeal, a persecutor of the church; as to righteousness under the law, blameless." He had the nerve to say that, as far as religious law was concerned, he was perfect. He had thought he did everything right.

Unfortunately, his zeal had been misdirected. In his letter to the Philippians, he allowed himself to be vulnerable and opened up about his sins.

When Paul wrote that "as to zeal, [he had been] a persecutor of the church," he meant that his religion had taught him to destroy Jewish Christians who no longer followed the Law of Moses. As a matter of fact, he had been taught not merely to persecute them, but to try to kill them.

His misguided view of his own credibility had come from religious performance, which created a false sense of hope, a false sense of importance, a false sense of accomplishment. These things about Paul had made him arrogant, divisive, unforgiving, and judgmental. He had produced criticism that was born of the evil one.

The religious dogs Paul spoke of at the beginning of Philippians 3 were not that different from the person he had been before he encountered Christ. Paul admitted that he had believed he was standing for truth while he persecuted the gospel. Instead, he stood for divisiveness.

However, Jesus turned Paul's world upside down. Paul was satisfied with his successful religious position, and he certainly wasn't seeking Jesus. Instead, Jesus sought and found Paul. And once he had been found by Christ, Paul treasured Him above all else.

Everything had been going Paul's way—the associations, the righteousness, the zealousness, the credibility. Suddenly, he completely changed his tune and called all that stuff a waste of his time, money, effort, and even his status.

Paul became, as he described in 2 Corinthians 5:17, a new creation in Christ. Knowing Jesus allowed Paul to see his past success with his religion as garbage. Instead, Paul's focus was now on the resurrected Christ, as he said in verse 7 of Philippians 3: "But whatever gain I had, I counted as loss for the sake of Christ." His focus shifted from religion to Christ.

When he saw Christ, Paul had a new goal. His focus was to please the Savior through righteousness and faith, not religious accomplishment. Try to grasp the magnitude of Paul's conversion from a religious expert to a follower of Christ. When Jesus saved him, it was so compelling that it caused Paul to say, "My religion is worthless; all I want is to know Jesus and the fellowship of His sufferings!"

Theology: Righteousness and Humble Confidence

Too many Christians have a warped perception of righteousness. They think of righteousness as a lifestyle choice, saying, "I'm going to live a righteous life."

I've got news for you: you will not be able to "live righteously," because righteousness is assigned to you; it is not earned. Understanding this is a key to learning how to live the GraceLife together with your church family.

Let me explain.

Jesus doesn't set forth a bunch of religious requirements that you must comply with to be in contact and connected with Him and our Heavenly Dad. Instead of writing out a list of dos and don'ts, Jesus took the religious burdens we will never live up to and bore the punishment we deserved. He became a religious failure in place of us, inviting us to cast our burdens on Him (Psalm 55:22).

He gathers our imperfections, including our religious failures, and takes them to the cross and the grave. In doing so, He takes His righteousness and puts it on us. We trade places with Jesus, who is perfectly righteous. He willingly takes our religious failure upon Himself so we can be identified with His spiritual perfection. He died a shameful death on the cross to pay for our sin and His righteousness was credited to us. Our perfectly holy God, in His judgment, cuts off the wicked (Proverbs 2:22), and Jesus chose to endure that punishment for us.

Instead of making us run the gauntlet of religious rules, Jesus ran it for us. He took our unrighteousness, He gave us His righteousness. And how much does this trade cost us? It's a gift. We pay nothing for it because Jesus paid everything for us.

This is what Paul meant when he declared his goal to "gain Christ and be found in him, not having a righteousness of my own that comes from the law, but that which comes through faith in Christ, the righteousness from God that depends on faith" (Philippians 3:8–9).

No person has righteousness of his or her own, but he or she can have the righteousness of Christ. The righteousness of God through faith is our only access to the blameless condition for eternal life with our Heavenly Dad. Christ does the religious work we're incapable of doing.

What exactly does this exchange do for us? Eternal life with Him, yes. But there's still more, and it's amazing. This exchange, righteousness for unrighteousness, gives us several things that are crucial to living the GraceLife together:

Righteousness Bathes Believers in Humility

Though our righteousness comes only through Christ, Christians sometimes brag about being righteous, which means that they are completely missing the point. Jesus did everything; we had nothing to do with the exchange of His righteousness for our sin. When the realization of being saved purely by what Jesus has done for us on the cross sinks in, there is an opportunity for us to be bathed in humility. In response to His amazing grace, we humbly worship at the feet of our great Savior.

Righteousness Allows Believers to Bask in Confidence

It seems impossible to say humility and confidence in the same breath. But doesn't it sound amazing? Christ takes our unrighteousness and gives us His own righteousness, and He takes our unrighteousness and dies with it. Now we have His righteousness, along with an amazing confidence in Christ's blood to save us from our sins. Christ has paid the price of my sin in full and made me righteous. I am free from the guilt of sin. So, while grace creates a reliant humility, it also infuses us with supernatural confidence!

Righteousness Enables the Elevation of Others

If your focus is on your own spiritual accomplishments that you believe make you righteous, then you will constantly be comparing your performance with those around you to gauge your progress. This can create an atmosphere of competition instead of an atmosphere of serving. However, when God gives you His righteousness, you can say, "I don't need to feel inferior in light of the accomplishments of others, because I'm basking in the confidence of the righteousness that was given to me for free."

Righteousness Empowers Believers

A righteousness we have not earned gives followers of Jesus the supernatural ability to offer genuine, sincere, and true words of exhortation to righteousness. We can approach hurting people with a powerful message of salvation rather than with words of criticism. We no longer need to push our own agenda, hoping that our listeners will conform to our thinking or measure up to hopeless

religious standards. Instead, we can boldly proclaim undeserved freedom in Christ, a freedom that is priceless
because it cost Him everything.

Righteousness Transforms

Religion desires conformity—as in, *here's our set of
rules and you better conform to them.* Grace, on the other
hand, desires transformation. Religious conformity happens temporarily, but transformation lasts for eternity.
The key to a transformed life is basking in humility as we
recognize that we are not righteous because of our own
merit but have been declared so by grace through faith.
The key to transformation is not an accomplished church.
It's faith. It's embracing the gift of grace and treasuring
Christ above all else.

Righteousness Helps Others Transform

When a person takes on the righteousness of God, that
person becomes a Kingdom agent commissioned to help
others transform. We are not trying to get them to conform
to a list of rules, we are saying, "Let me tell you how I
became righteous. It had nothing to do with me. It was all
about the work of Christ." Now we can be armed with a
real gospel, along with our testimony of what God has
done for us, and turn outward, helping others to know the
transforming power of Jesus.

This is what God did for Paul! Before his encounter
with Christ, Paul was killing the church. Once God saved
him, Paul planted churches and told everyone he talked to

about Christ. And in our passage, he was under house arrest, facing the possibility of death, and all he could think about was his love for the Philippians. He experienced tremendous suffering, but his focus was on loving others and helping them to grow in their faith. Paul longed to see the Philippians transformed by the amazing grace that changed his own life and led him to proclaim the supreme worth of Jesus.

Humble Confidence

I've been playing basketball for years. Sometimes I'm a good jump shooter, and I'll hit a few great shots in a row. But then a thought in my head takes over—"I'm shooting so well today. The next time I get the ball, and somebody comes running at me, I'm going to blow a kiss to the guy defending me and take the shot."

Here's the problem: over the course of my basketball career, when I shoot while puckering up my lips, my success rate is about eight percent. My boasting has an uncanny way of undermining any success I might otherwise have had.

We are tempted to put ourselves up on a pedestal and blow a kiss to the rest of the world. We see our works, and Jesus' blessings, and we sometimes start thinking, "I like where I am right now. I'm going to church more often. I'm volunteering, I'm helping. Gosh, I'm an exemplary Christian!" and we are tempted to blow a kiss spiritually.

Confidence in ourselves is like building a house on a swamp. In contrast, humble confidence in Jesus is like building a house on a foundation of rock.

Writing to the Corinthian church, Paul declared:

All this is from God, who through Christ reconciled us to himself and gave us the ministry of reconciliation; that is, in Christ God was reconciling the world to himself, not counting their trespasses against them, and entrusting to us the message of reconciliation. Therefore, we are ambassadors for Christ, God making his appeal through us. We implore you on behalf of Christ, be reconciled to God. For our sake he made him to be sin who knew no sin, so that in him we might become the righteousness of God.
—*2 Corinthians 5:18–21*

Once made righteous, Paul said, followers of Jesus are "ambassadors for Christ" and God is "making his appeal through us." Jesus, the One who knew no sin, became sin, so that we could become righteous before God. This is grace, and this is what brings humble confidence, which is necessary to live the GraceLife together.

My religious expertise will not allow me to love others; only God's righteousness in me can accomplish that. My humble confidence rests in the fact that God has saved my wretched, dirty, sinful soul and is transforming me by the power of His grace and the blood of Christ.

Devotional: Living with Humble Confidence

Our humble confidence is founded in the great exchange at the cross, where our unrighteousness was taken away and His righteousness was given to us. The process starts with our brokenness.

The stark reality is, even though I am a pastor, I am

extremely bad at following religious rules. However, I am extremely good at needing and accepting grace and mercy and forgiveness!

Our humble confidence is in the power of our faith, and even that is not of us. Our faith is a gift that transforms us by His Word and His Spirit. Our humble confidence is a powerful agent for changing others, because our confidence to impact others starts with realizing that our personal success is, as Paul calls it, "dung." It's really no better than garbage.

Paul had confidence enough to pastor the Philippians and start Gentile churches all across the region because he realized that, compared to Christ, everything else is garbage.

Some religious people are only capable of deadly salvos that destroy relationships, destroy unity, and destroy lives. We judge a marriage in crisis, criticize a single mom struggling to discipline her children, and look down on someone struggling in recovery from addiction. We do these things, and many more, without understanding and loving people right where they are in their lives. As Jesus said:

Woe to you, scribes and Pharisees, hypocrites! For you are like whitewashed tombs, which outwardly appear beautiful, but within are full of dead people's bones and all uncleanness. So you also outwardly appear righteous to others, but within you are full of hypocrisy and lawlessness.

—Matthew 23:27–28

But humble confidence gives us credibility because our

confidence is based upon brokenness, humility, grace, forgiveness, and mercy, not our position on the spiritual ladder. Isn't that awesome?

When you step into the world with faith, you are no longer a religious failure, but you possess the very righteousness of God. Because of brokenness and humility, you have been entrusted with the ministry of reconciliation, and you can have all the amazing, inspiring, humble confidence necessary to boldly impact others, not because you're good at it, but because you know God works in spite of you, not because of you.

We are so bad at religion, but thank God, Jesus is good at grace. Through humble confidence, we can confront people with grace and mercy, even while being colossal religious failures, and we ourselves become a tool for transformation and change. This is a key to how we spread the concept of the GraceLife to those around us.

WORKBOOK

Chapter Seven Questions

Question: What does the Bible mean by "righteousness"? Why does religion fall short of the righteousness that is yours by faith in Jesus Christ? Does this mean you no longer need to obey any religious laws or commandments? Why or why not?

_____

_____

_____

_____

_____

_____

_____

_____

_____

_____

100 · JOSEPH DAVIS

_____

_____

Question: What is "humble confidence"? What is a specific example of this in action? How does humble confidence lead to a ministry of reconciliation?

_____

_____

_____

_____

_____

_____

_____

_____

_____

_____

_____

Action: Paul listed his previous achievements that he once believed qualified him for righteousness. Write down anything that could set you above other people. Do you find yourself referring to your background, ministry, or calling? Can you truly say you consider it all as garbage compared to knowing Jesus? Ask God to show you where you are still holding onto these things instead of humbly relying on His righteousness alone.

Pray:

> Heavenly Dad, we are overwhelmed when we look at the measuring stick of religion. We're overwhelmed at just how bad we are at it. And then we are so comforted by how good You are at working in spite of that anyway, taking our colossal religious failures and giving us this ministry of reconciliation.
>
> God, help us today with humble confidence that there is no one we cannot confront with grace, even when needing it desperately ourselves.

Chapter Seven Notes

CHAPTER EIGHT

Supernatural Perseverance

Not that I have already obtained this or am already perfect, but I press on to make it my own, because Christ Jesus has made me his own. Brothers, I do not consider that I have made it my own. But one thing I do: forgetting what lies behind and straining forward to what lies ahead, I press on toward the goal for the prize of the upward call of God in Christ Jesus. Let those of us who are mature think this way, and if in anything you think otherwise, God will reveal that also to you. Only let us hold true to what we have attained.

Brothers, join in imitating me, and keep your eyes on those who walk according to the example you have in us. For many, of whom I have often told you and now tell you even with tears, walk as enemies of the cross of Christ. Their end is destruction, their god is their belly, and they glory in their shame, with minds set on earthly things. But our citizenship is in heaven, and from it we await a Savior, the Lord Jesus Christ, who will transform our lowly body to be like his glorious body, by the power that enables him even to subject all things to himself.

—Philippians 3:12–21

Perseverance is a crucial part of being able to live the

GraceLife together with our church family. If we are surrounded by people who get discouraged easily and give up quickly, it is more difficult to stay motivated, loyal, sacrificial, and committed to them. Without the perseverance of its members, the church is nothing more than a transient club. In this chapter, we will study both the perseverance of Paul and that of the Philippians to demonstrate how crucial an ingredient it was in their special relationship.

History: What Kept Paul Going?

Paul displayed amazing endurance in his ministry. He was persecuted by Jews who wanted to kill him and persecuted by pagans for taking people away from their false religions. And now, as he endured house arrest, both of these groups were likely very glad he was no longer able to roam freely.

But Paul had made a commitment to the Philippians that he would never ever turn his back on them. And without doubt, he would never turn his back on the gospel of Jesus. He was locked in.

Consider the following questions:

- Do you think the Philippians were inspired by Paul's endurance?

- Do you think that Paul was motivated to persevere because he had taught the Philippians the gospel and they had stayed true to Jesus?

- Do you think the Philippians' obedience and

faithfulness encouraged Paul?

- Can you imagine the impact if Paul had given up on the Philippians or the gospel?

The Philippians knew Paul was credible. He was a reliable, steadfast, honest ally who would never, ever change. Thus, when Paul was under house arrest, facing the possibility of death, they knew they could trust him even more. Paul didn't turn his back on the Philippians at this moment of crisis; he was committed to their growth and committed to encouraging them in their walk—which would face trials and tribulations as well.

The Philippians were not amazing people from a special gene pool that made them faithful. They were sinners, just like us. They were people struggling in their marriages, struggling with money, struggling with recovery, or their jobs, or their spirituality.

Paul wasn't some superstar who was better than we are, either.

Yet, somehow, Paul and the Philippians had an amazing, supernatural perseverance. And do you know why? Because their faith was steadfast. Lasting. Their faith, which came from Heavenly Dad, was irreversible.

And the endurance that came from their supernatural faith produced this supernatural perseverance, allowing them to feed off each other. A positive faith feedback loop provides great encouragement for believers today and gives us insight into how and why Paul could write this powerfully.

Theology: Supernatural Perseverance

Let me explain to you what supernatural perseverance looks like when God has given someone the gift of faith (Ephesians 2:8–9).

Those who persevere have a supernatural yearning. Paul wrote in Philippians 3:12–13:

> *Not that I have already obtained this or am already perfect, but I press on to make it my own, because Christ Jesus has made me his own. Brothers, I do not consider that I have made it my own. But one thing I do: forgetting what lies behind and straining forward to what lies ahead...*

Inside of real faith is a yearning which drives Christians to something deeper, something better. No matter how appealing the spiritual mountaintop may seem, if you have been given the gift of faith, you know there is something better, something closer to God than anything you're looking at right now.

In Matthew 17:1–3, Jesus and the disciples journeyed up a literal mountain. Scripture says:

> *And after six days Jesus took with him Peter and James, and John his brother, and led them up a high mountain by themselves. And he was transfigured before them, and his face shone like the sun, and his clothes became white as light. And behold, there appeared to them Moses and Elijah, talking with them.*

Next, Peter said to Jesus, "Lord, it is good that we are

here. If you wish, I will make three tents here, one for you and one for Moses and one for Elijah" (Matthew 17:4).

Jesus essentially told him, "No, you can't stay right here. This is nothing."

When you're living life and things are great, you're on a mountaintop. Sometimes, believers have a mountaintop experience and think, "This is it!" But if you have been given the gift of faith, even when things are going well, there's still a yearning inside for more. And when you're struggling, there's even more of a yearning.

It's like a little child on the floor reaching up for his or her mommy or daddy. That's exactly the way children of God are when it comes to our yearning for Heavenly Dad. We are reaching, but we have not yet reached. We are being perfected, but we are not yet perfect. Even when there are valleys, faith enables us to press on and not fall in love with a mountaintop. We're reaching past mountaintops to be with God.

Supernatural perseverance also involves growth. Real faith will not allow you to be stagnant in your walk with Jesus. In Philippians 3:13, Paul said that he was "forgetting what lies behind and straining forward to what lies ahead." He was saying, "I'm determined because of the gift of faith. I continue on. Yes, I helped plant the church in Philippi and it's going great, but I'm going to keep going." We are determined. We are focused on the goal.

We can "do" church really well, but if we're not focused on the right direction, it doesn't matter. It's like a top golfer driving the ball 375 yards to the wrong hole.

We work really hard to make sure that our swing is beautiful, but sometimes we're not going in the right direction.

If a church is preaching the gospel of Jesus, it will have the right goal. It will shoot in the right direction. The problem is that sometimes believers forget the fundamentals, such as the fact that we are saved by grace through faith, not by works. It is ironic, because often we equate growth with amassing more knowledge. Of course, growing in the knowledge of Christ and His truth is beneficial, but growth and perseverance will cease if we leave the foundations of our faith.

Hebrews 5:11–12 affirms this. The author was writing to a church that was well educated but had forgotten the basics of the gospel:

> *About this we have much to say, and it is hard to explain, since you have become dull of hearing. For though by this time you ought to be teachers, you need someone to teach you again the basic principles of the oracles of God. You need milk, not solid food.*

Staying true to the fundamentals was the core of what gave Paul endurance. Like him, if we are to persevere, we must never forget the foundation. That foundation, the gospel of Jesus Christ, is what enables us to strive for, and long for, a deeper relationship with God and with each other. If we ever think we have moved beyond the gospel, considering ourselves too sophisticated or knowledgeable for it, we have gone too far.

Further, the gift of faith provides perseverance that

transforms us into people who are worthy to be imitated. Paul encouraged the Philippians to imitate him as he imitated Christ (Philippians 3:17). Paul wasn't being arrogant, because he had said earlier, "I do not consider that I have made it my own" (Philippians 3:13). The result of the gift of faith is a life that is enduring, inspiring, and worthy to be imitated.

Hebrews 12:1–2 says:

> Therefore, since we are surrounded by so great a cloud of witnesses, let us also lay aside every weight, and sin which clings so closely, and let us run with endurance the race that is set before us, looking to Jesus, the founder and perfecter of our faith, who for the joy that was set before him endured the cross, despising the shame, and is seated at the right hand of the throne of God.

The scripture here says when we see people who have been transformed—people whose lives are changing—their perseverance is contagious, and we want to imitate them. While no one is perfect, there should be some aspects of your life that other people can look at and say, "Wow, I want to be like that!"

Finally, the last ingredient of supernatural perseverance is hope. Real faith enables us to be forward-looking people, because faith assures us that the future is better than anything the past or present has to offer. That's hope. And that's why Paul discussed "forgetting those things which are behind, and reaching forth unto those things which are before" (Philippians 3:13 KJV).

Now, the past—hard times that we went through, good times that we enjoyed, the times that we had victory in our lives—can certainly still encourage us. The victories we experience when we struggle and God brings people into our lives to help us heal are great reminders of God's presence, but they aren't the end.

We can hope that our faith will do something even greater than it has done in the past. That's why Scripture says, "Now faith is the substance of things hoped for, the evidence of things not seen" (Hebrews 11:1 KJV). Moreover, "he who began a good work in you will bring it to completion at the day of Jesus Christ" (Philippians 1:6).

Paul, writing to the Corinthians, described why the believer hopes:

> So we do not lose heart. Though our outer self is wasting away, our inner self is being renewed day by day. For this light momentary affliction is preparing for us an eternal weight of glory beyond all comparison, as we look not to the things that are seen but to the things that are unseen. For the things that are seen are transient, but the things that are unseen are eternal.
> —*2 Corinthians 4:16–18*

This world offers the believer trials, illnesses, disease, heartache, hurt, and betrayal. As we endure through these difficult, and often temporary, struggles, we can have confidence that our faith will make us glorious. We yearn and long for that time. This is the hope that is crucial to our supernatural perseverance together through the good and the bad of our earthly lives. Through the gift of faith, we press forward with confidence that the end result, which is glorification, will exceed our wildest imaginations.

Devotional: Living with Supernatural Perseverance

Supernatural perseverance is a crucial part of the GraceLife. However, there are trials that can serve to derail and discourage us from the GraceLife and hinder our perseverance. In fact, the lowest time in my life, which I shared with you earlier in this book, was the greatest, most powerful spiritual experience because I was able to actually live out supernatural perseverance that made no earthly sense.

Supernatural perseverance means we will never quit on each other, even when we want to. How many times have you said the phrase, "Oh, I am so done," but then somehow found the faith to keep going? I have been "so done" with church dozens of times. I've hurt people. People have hurt me. But the gift of faith that God gave me when I was a freshman in high school has given me this supernatural perseverance. I will continue to stick with the church, and the church will stick with me. I will cling to the gospel—the gospel will never leave me. And I will be with Heavenly Dad and my family one day in heaven—for eternity.

There are denominational disagreements, criticism from loved ones, disappointments and unmet expectations. Sometimes the trials are understandable and fair, as if they were consequences for our actions, but often they feel unfair. Either way, trials and tribulations are not fun. And as we saw earlier, bad theology and straying from the foundation of the gospel can interrupt the GraceLife by attempting to derail our supernatural perseverance.

Sometimes money can be a distraction, both when there is too much and when there is not enough. Likewise, interpersonal and political conflicts, inside and outside the church, can steal away our supernatural perseverance. Too often, our own personal failures shake our confidence, destroy relationships, and rob us of the joys of the GraceLife.

However, faith gives us humble confidence because we are not required to trust in accomplishing religious to-do lists. Faith enables us to have endurance and stay in the fight shoulder to shoulder, knowing that we can look over during difficult times and find that we are not alone, that we are with others who display supernatural perseverance because of the gift of faith.

Faith allows us to see God keeping the body of Christ close around us, and that is where we find inspiration, motivation, courage, and a second wind when life weighs us down. Faith feeds on itself, growing stronger in faith-filled churches. Of course, as individuals and as a church, we're going to get things wrong and conflicts and issues will ensue. But supernatural perseverance, which is a by-product of faith, will force us at some point to squash these conflicts.

Have confidence in this: I may let you down, but God, in whom our faith resides, will not. In theology class, this truth is tied to the concept called *perseverance of the saints*. The reality that God empowers those He has called to follow Him until the end is both supernatural and unbelievably inspirational as you watch it play out among your brothers and sisters who are living the GraceLife with you.

So, if you're feeling a little winded, look around you. You're not alone. When you feel like you are on the mountaintop, look around. Someone else might be in a valley. And together, as we look at what God is doing in each other's lives, we will be overcome with God's strength to persevere.

WORKBOOK

Chapter Eight Questions

Question: Have you ever experienced a relationship of mutual encouragement and perseverance, such as the one Paul and the Philippians had? How did it inspire you to press forward in times of difficulty?

_____

_____

_____

_____

_____

_____

_____

_____

_____

_____

Question: What personal struggles have you experienced that have shaken your confidence? How have you found supernatural perseverance to keep hoping and believing?

_____

_____

_____

_____

_____

_____

_____

_____

_____

_____

_____

Action: Take a few moments to consider what qualities in your life might inspire those around you. Choose a few trusted Christian friends and ask them for a character assessment. The result may surprise or even dismay you, but God can use all of us. Ask Him to show you how you can be a blessing to others.

Chapter Eight Notes

CHAPTER NINE

Just Call Me Coach

*Therefore, my brothers, whom I love and long for, my joy
and crown, stand firm thus in the Lord, my beloved. I entreat
Euodia and I entreat Syntyche to agree in the Lord. Yes, I ask
you also, true companion, help these women, who have la-
bored side by side with me in the gospel together with
Clement and the rest of my fellow workers, whose names
are in the book of life.*

*Rejoice in the Lord always; again I will say, rejoice. Let your
reasonableness be known to everyone. The Lord is at hand;
do not be anxious about anything, but in everything by
prayer and supplication with thanksgiving let your requests
be made known to God. And the peace of God, which surpasses all understanding, will guard your hearts and your
minds in Christ Jesus.*

*Finally, brothers, whatever is true, whatever is honorable,
whatever is just, whatever is pure, whatever is lovely, whatever is commendable, if there is any excellence, if there is
anything worthy of praise, think about these things. What
you have learned and received and heard and seen in me—
practice these things, and the God of peace will be with you.*
—Philippians 4:1–9

Coaching, in a wide variety of settings, has been a huge part of my life. I coached high school football for about fifteen years and high school basketball on and off for about twenty years. I've grown tremendously in this role, and I've learned so much about myself and about how to take care of and minister to others. As a matter of fact, I cut my teeth ministering specifically to young people through coaching.

A coach can inspire a team more than anyone else. He's with the players every minute of the season. He's there through the successes and the failures. He feels their pain and defeat. He feels the thrill of victory when they win. He has an ability to inspire them like no one else can.

With that in mind, I want to examine a pregame speech that Paul gave to the Philippians 4:1–9. This passage provides a great example of exhortation and coaching. Let's first understand the historical context of this passage before delving deeper.

History: Coach Paul

First and foremost, Paul offered step-by-step instructions for believers to mature and for churches to go to the next level.

He didn't say, "Hey listen, I want you to be a good church. Good luck with that. I'm going to go start another one." He spent time with them, side by side, saying, "Look, here's the next step. I see you have a problem here, and I want you to fix it," or, "That was an amazing job, and I'm really proud of the example you are to the rest of the churches. I'm going to tell them about what you did."

He told them, to paraphrase and expand on Ephesians 2:10, "Here's how the gospel works. Here's how you interact with people who are Jewish. Here's how you interact with people who are pagan. Here's how you should interact with people who are Christians." And on he went, step by step.

In his letter to the Philippians, Paul moved from warning believers to "Look out for the dogs, look out for the evildoers, look out for those who mutilate the flesh" (Philippians 3:2) to admonishing them for fighting (Philippians 4:2). His rebukes remind me of wind sprints at the end of football practice. They cause players temporary discomfort that passes quickly and leads to greater unity as a team. Paul's admonishments serve a similar function in this passage, causing pain that is needed prior to further progress.

Once the necessary "wind sprints" of admonishment were finished, Paul moved on to let the church at Philippi know what he believed their next steps should be. In Philippians 4:6, he instructed the Philippians not to be anxious but to pray about everything. Paul told them that, as they continued growing together, the peace of God that surpasses all understanding would guard their hearts and minds (verse 7). And in verse 8, he told them to consider what is honorable and just and pure.

Because he was so intimately familiar with the church at Philippi, Coach Paul knew all of this and carefully helped the Philippians to understand. His ability to lead them came from being side by side with them, just as a good coach would be with his team.

Theology: Exhortation

The Greek word for *exhortation* in this passage is *para-kalo*. There are two words that make up the Greek word. The first one is *para*, meaning "close beside."[6] We get the word *parallel* from it. The word *exhortation* therefore implies being in close proximity—that is, close beside the recipient of your exhortation.

You cannot exhort someone you've never met, or know little about, with raw information on trust, specifics, foundation and purpose, and instruction. Few people will listen to advice outside of a relationship based on trust.

The second word is *kalo*.[7] It means "to call." So, literally, exhortation means to call someone from close beside them.

When you walk next to somebody, you do not need to yell to be heard when you speak into that person's life. This is what Paul was doing in Philippians 4—exhortation.

If there are no examples in your life of being an exhorter or a coach to others, you have reason to question your spirituality, and even whether you've been given the gift of faith. This is not to suggest that you earn your salvation through coaching or exhorting others. However, if you have been given the gift of faith, one of the natural results is that you are a coach to some degree to someone, somehow, because God never does a bad job of giving the gift of faith.

Now, there are several important aspects of exhortation. Let's look at the key points.

Trust

A key for exhortation and coaching is a relationship of trust. Paul acknowledged that he had been with the Philippians for a long time, and a level of trust had developed between them. This is a crucial element in any coaching situation. If there is no trust in a mentoring relationship, the person who attempts to exhort is perceived as merely criticizing and judging.

Trust comes from an established relationship. If the coach knows the recipient of the advice well, the coach is able to be creative, since he or she knows what motivates and encourages the recipient. The coach must show that he or she is invested in the recipient's success, not just his or her own.

Specifics

It is also very important for the coach to be aware of the specifics of each unique situation. Otherwise, it is difficult to give direction and measure success. If a coach is not sensitive to the specifics, the person receiving counsel can be overwhelmed by the suggested goal. "Okay, Joe, here's what I want you to do. Go start a church. I'll drop by later to tell you whether or not you did a good job." I couldn't have followed that advice.

Coaching and exhortation turn into discouragement if the specifics are not taken into consideration. Moreover, exhortation not grounded in the specifics of the situation is pointless. For example, it is unwise to go to someone who can't draw and tell that person to create a new church logo. You have to be able to understand the specifics that apply to the person involved and consider the strengths and weaknesses of that particular individual.

Foundation and Purpose

There's another ingredient in exhortation and coaching that's crucial: the discourse must have a solid foundation and purpose. In other words, there needs to be substance to the message that is given.

Imagine for a minute that I am a highly-paid motivational speaker coming to talk to you. I walk in, you laugh, you smile, and you have a great time. Some of you cry. You pay me a couple hundred thousand dollars. And then I'm out of there.

But there's no foundation laid. It's just an empty talk.

It is also essential for good coaching to spell out and explain desired results. If a coach doesn't provide an end goal, a purpose, then that person will have a hard time finding the motivation to do his or her best work.

If I'm coaching a player, I need to explain the purpose and the foundation, otherwise there's no understanding or motivation. Paul offered his purpose in Philippians 4:7 when he said that if the Philippians did all of these things, the peace of God that surpasses all understanding would be with them.

Instruction

The last element necessary for exhortation and coaching is detailed instruction. When I coached, if I asked a player to do something before I taught him or her how to do it, the results were either embarrassing, dangerous, or both.

Let's say I want someone to change his or her behavior and I tell him or her, "You've got to do this and if you do, this is what will happen. Now, I'm going to check back with you in thirty days."

Instruction of this kind isn't helpful. There must be steps that detail exactly what the person being counseled is supposed to do. Paul spelled out his instructions clearly in his letter to the Philippians.

In summary, it is important to note that all these elements were present in Paul's coaching relationship with the Philippians: There was trust. There were specifics. There was a foundation and purpose, and there were detailed instructions.

Devotional: Exhorting and Coaching One Another

God calls believers to be coaching and exhorting each other frequently. It's a crucial part of the GraceLife. We must strive to earn the right to coach one another and extend the privilege of letting others coach us. The writer of Hebrews said, "But exhort one another every day, as long as it is called 'today,' that none of you may be hardened by the deceitfulness of sin" (Hebrews 3:13).

We are to come close beside other believers daily to prevent the body from becoming hardened by the deceitfulness of sin.

"Every day" requires us to be together regularly and consistently. The coaching and motivation and encouragement found in deep, intimate, vulnerable relationships won't happen without daily presence. If we don't have examples of coaching in our lives, the church might as well not meet, because this is part of what makes Christians different. This is part of what makes living the GraceLife so dynamic.

As discussed previously, *parakalo* means calling out from close beside someone.[8] And that's why I hope we can each say to our brothers and sisters who are hurting, "You can call me coach."

Please understand that exhortation and coaching are different from accountability. As we discussed earlier, accountability is vital. You have to earn the right to hold others accountable, and you must allow others to earn the right to hold you accountable.

While accountability, exhortation, and coaching do go hand and hand, working together, each is different. Exhortation and coaching are the missing links that take people from knowledge to action. That is why they are so important in so many aspects of life, especially in the church.

Here's the part I like: *Teaching targets the mind, but exhortation and coaching are focused squarely on the heart!* The very nature of exhortation, *parakalo*, means that the individuals are side by side.

We must realize that, without good relationships, there will be no coaching. And as a church, there will be no action. Intimate relationships create accountability, so we may coach one another. There is no better example of the value of these types of relationships than that of Paul and the Philippians.

Have you ever noticed the farther away you are from a person, the more demonstrative you must be to give them instruction? The greater the distance, the louder you have to yell.

James explained this in his New Testament letter. He said, "What causes quarrels and what causes fights among you? Is it not this, that your passions are at war within you?" (James 4:1). In other words: "You are not close to each other. You are just looking to fulfill your own lusts and desires."

Coaches will take the time to invest in you and come close beside you. I have found times in my life where my ministry and my walk with Jesus were flourishing. I noticed that I was not walking alone at those times, and someone had taken the time out of his or her busy schedule to spend precious moments with me, to help me grow, to help me through my struggles. At the times when I was hurting, when I was in pain or I had lost my way, when I felt like I had lost my calling, they were there to help guide and comfort me.

God has put exhorters, or coaches, in my life. They know who they are because I have told them so. I trust them. When they talk to me, they speak right to my heart and into my soul. They calm my fears and promise to be there with a helping hand when needed. They have spurred me on with courage and confidence to do what seems to be too big and too risky and too scary. But this exhortation and coaching only happened because these individuals were truly interested in our success as a church. They are living the GraceLife together, side by side with me.

This concept is such an important ingredient of the GraceLife that I will tell you again: if you find you never really exhort or coach others, there is a good chance that you don't have the love of the brethren in you and therefore might not even love Jesus. A church must be a community, bursting at the seams with instances of coaching and exhortation at every level. Deep, intimate, vulnerable relationships foster an environment where coaching, motivation, and encouragement abound. This is what makes living the GraceLife so powerful, attractive, and dynamic.

Chapter Nine Questions

Question: Think of someone who has successfully coached you, whether in sports, academics, or spiritual matters. What made that person a great coach? Why were you willing to listen to him or her?

_____

_____

_____

_____

_____

_____

_____

_____

_____

_____

Question: How does exhortation form the missing link between knowledge and action? Why is it necessary to lay a foundation and not merely to give instructions? What is an example you've experienced personally of spiritual knowledge failing to translate into action? How exactly might exhortation have affected this situation?

_____

_____

_____

_____

_____

_____

_____

_____

_____

_____

Action: Thank God for the people in your life who have coached you to help you grow and develop. Ask Him to show you how to come alongside others and exhort them. Who do you know who could use a helping hand as he or she learns more about God's love?

Chapter Nine Notes

_____

_____

_____

_____

_____

_____

_____

_____

_____

_____

_____

_____

_____

_____

_____

_____

_____

_____

_____

_____

_____

_____

CHAPTER TEN

Living in Gratitude

I rejoiced in the Lord greatly that now at length you have revived your concern for me. You were indeed concerned for me, but you had no opportunity. Not that I am speaking of being in need, for I have learned in whatever situation I am to be content. I know how to be brought low, and I know how to abound. In any and every circumstance, I have learned the secret of facing plenty and hunger, abundance and need. I can do all things through him who strengthens me.

Yet it was kind of you to share my trouble. And you Philippians yourselves know that in the beginning of the gospel, when I left Macedonia, no church entered into partnership with me in giving and receiving, except you only. Even in Thessalonica you sent me help for my needs once and again. Not that I seek the gift, but I seek the fruit that increases to your credit. I have received full payment, and more. I am well supplied, having received from Epaphroditus the gifts you sent, a fragrant offering, a sacrifice acceptable and pleasing to God. And my God will supply every need of yours according to his riches in glory in Christ Jesus. To our God and Father be glory forever and ever. Amen.

Greet every saint in Christ Jesus. The brothers who are with me greet you. All the saints greet you, especially those of

Caesar's household. The grace of the Lord Jesus Christ be with your spirit.

—Philippians 4:10–23

Have you ever received an encouraging letter from someone who knows you well? The person writing it knows you and writes about specific things that mean a lot to both of you. Whether it comes through the mail, is handed to you, or arrives in your email inbox, the note is heartfelt and genuine. It might even bring a tear to your eye. Either way, you won't soon forget what it contained or how it made you feel.

Thankfulness and *gratitude* are often used interchangeably, but they are, at their deepest levels, very different indeed.

History: Paul Living in Gratitude

Several examples exist of how Paul lived in gratitude toward the Philippians. The Philippians had helped him out when he had nothing (Philippians 4:15), and while he was thankful for this specific action, Paul had an ongoing posture of gratitude toward them. He *lived* in gratitude. It was part of his GraceLife.

We see that Paul was grateful to the Philippians for their intentions as well as for their actions. He said, "I rejoiced in the Lord greatly that now at length you have revived your concern for me. You were indeed concerned for me, but you had no opportunity" (Philippians 4:10).

Sometimes we hold back our gratitude, living out proverbial sayings such as "The proof is in the pudding" or

"Show me first." However, Paul was always grateful regardless of whether anything was given to him, because he knew that the Philippians desired to bless him even when circumstances prevented them from helping. He trusted their overall intentions even when they could not be manifested through actions. Their concern alone was a sufficient reason for his gratitude.

We see that Paul also expressed gratitude when he was suffering, and not just when he was blessed or relieved from suffering. Paul's gratitude was independent of life circumstances, whether they were really bad or really good.

Moreover, Paul was not only grateful for the present but also for the past. In Philippians 4:14–16, he talked about the time when he left Macedonia and no other church was supporting him except the church in Philippi. You see, without grace, human nature tends to remember the past to justify anger or bitterness. But living a life of gratitude enables you to remember the past in a way that creates love.

If anybody could have justification for the past making him bitter, it would have been Paul. And I'll share this: if you have a long memory for mistakes and a short memory for blessings, there's a lack of gratitude in your life and a lack of understanding of grace.

Paul was also grateful for anything he received. Sometimes he had plenty and sometimes he had nothing. Whether he was living in abundance or in dire need, he would humbly receive gifts in the same manner.

Often, people have a hard time receiving, and the root cause lies in arrogance. Paul was saying, "I didn't need anything, but I accepted your gift, knowing that you will be blessed through the process of participating and sharing."

Those who live with gratitude recognize the hand of God in the life of the person who's trying to bless them. All our resources belong to Him anyway, and if He wants to give you something through someone else, who are you not to take it?

The last thing Paul did was to live in gratitude in a way that fostered affection. In Philippians 4:15, Paul's gratitude was simply an acknowledgement, an encouragement to them. Do you see how powerful that can be? When someone shows gratitude for part of my life and how it blessed his or her own, it makes my heart soar. Imagine how the Philippians felt. "You know that time when I was leaving Macedonia? You were the only ones who helped." Can you see how that would have been encouraging to them?

Theology: Gratitude, a Result of Grace

The Greek word for *thanksgiving* in Philippians 4:6 is *eucharistia*, which can also be translated as *gratitude*[9] The prefix is *eu-*, meaning "good."[10] The middle of the word is *charis*, which literally means "grace."[11] Right smack in the middle of the word *gratitude*, therefore, is this idea of undeserved favor—grace. Living in gratitude means living in good grace.

Paul's example, set in Philippians 4, was living in good

grace with the Philippians. It wasn't only about thankfulness.

Gratitude has a very close relationship to grace. You can't experience true gratitude without first receiving grace through faith, because grace, which is undeserved favor from God, produces humility. And humility is necessary for a lifestyle of gratitude.

If you've tasted forgiveness, if you really have experienced cleansing, healing, and grace, if you have the blessing of adoption where Jesus Christ takes you from being a child of darkness and a child of sin and transforms you into a child of light, you will have a new nature that allows you to live in gratitude with others.

Change your perspective and change your concept of gratitude. Thankfulness is founded in your own desires being fulfilled, but Paul had gratitude even when his desires weren't being fulfilled.

Our natural tendency is to think God is favoring us when things go well—"Oh, I'm so thankful and so blessed by God with all these things that He has given me." But there are believers around the world, godlier than you and me, who are just trying to figure out how they're going to eat. Can they live in gratitude?

Yes, because gratitude is not a reaction to good things or pleasant circumstances. It isn't simply little moments of thankfulness. Gratitude is acknowledging God's presence in your life. It's acknowledging God's presence in others and then extending His grace to others.

Often, Philippians 4:13 is misinterpreted to mean that the believer can accomplish anything through Christ: "I can do all things through him who strengthens me." The passage doesn't mean that at all. Paul was not teaching the Philippian believers about accomplishment but about contentment. It's not a verse about motivation; instead, it's a verse about filtering life through grace. Gratitude is intimately linked with grace, as the following personal story illustrates.

For a time, I was in South Carolina as a youth pastor in a suburban church. We had a conflict in which a girl was going to our youth group and her parents were going to another church. Her parents' church was a big one downtown, where the pastor was an older man with three doctoral degrees. I was about twenty-seven or twenty-eight. I called up the pastor, and I started telling him all the things he was doing wrong with this family. I just laid it out for him, boom, boom, boom, boom. And he listened and said, "Thank you, Joe, I appreciate you. I'll take that under advisement."

I responded with, "All right, good, I'm glad to hear I got through to you." I hung up the phone, and about ten minutes later, I thought, "I'm an idiot. This guy has been in ministry for decades." I called him back and said, "Listen, Pastor, I just realized what I did. I ranted for fifteen minutes and you just listened and thanked me. Why?"

And he said, "Joe, I understood why you were calling. You're a shepherd. You love the people in your church. So, everything you said, I knew I could filter through grace."

His response and the love that was behind it changed my life. His reaction was a picture of what it means to filter life through grace. He was a man who lived in gratitude, even when I mistreated him.

Devotional: Living a Grateful Life

Start today, right now, to live a life of gratitude like Paul. Don't just be thankful briefly and forget about the occasion after having said thank you once. Being grateful means always remembering what was done for you and understanding that you cannot live on your own, without God's grace and fellowship with God's children.

Thankfulness can be fleeting, but gratitude never ends. It's recognizing that God is using people in your life to transform you, to challenge you, to change you. Gratitude is a key pinnacle of living the GraceLife together.

When your cup of life is filled with gratitude, there is very little room for impatience, anger, bitterness, or unforgiveness. You cannot be living a life of gratitude and have all these negative attitudes dominating you every day.

True gratitude is a lifestyle of giving and receiving grace, not just from God but from each other. Grace produces humility, generosity, compassion, and forgiveness—all evidence of a life of gratitude.

I encourage you to begin and end your day by remembering all the things that you can be grateful for—not just things that happened that day, but over the entire course of your life. I also encourage you to take the time to thank God and others regularly for the things you are grateful for.

WORKBOOK

Chapter Ten Questions

Question: What are the two Greek words that make up the word *gratitude*? What are the differences between gratitude and thankfulness? Why is it important to remember the past and deal with the present in a way that promotes love? What is an example you've personally experienced of filtering life through grace?

_____

_____

_____

_____

_____

_____

_____

_____

_____

_____

_____

Question: It is easy to be grateful when things are going your way. How, specifically, can you develop a lifestyle of giving and receiving grace when circumstances are more difficult?

_____

_____

_____

_____

_____

_____

_____

_____

_____

_____

Action: Practice living a life of gratitude by starting a gratitude journal. Make a point of writing down every day the things for which you are grateful, and praise God for His blessings. Note the name of anyone who's helped you recently and make a point of thanking him or her.

Chapter Ten Notes

_____

_____

_____

_____

_____

_____

_____

_____

_____

_____

_____

_____

_____

_____

_____

_____

_____

_____

_____

_____

CONCLUSION

Live It Well

We took a special approach in going through this study of Philippians. We first looked at the history and the theology of each passage before delving into the devotional, or practical, application. I hope this helped you to understand and internalize the messages in these passages.

Through studying the relationship between Paul and his favorite church, I pray that you have a better picture of what the GraceLife looks like and numerous practical applications that can help you to live more like Christ.

Remember that, first and foremost, you are saved by grace. The church is called to suffer together and be blessed by it! We must love each other humbly and relentlessly. We are to hold others accountable with affection, beware of religious dogs that seek to pull us from the truth, and stand strong in mercy rather than religion. And, when we tap into God's supernatural perseverance to help us do all these things, we develop a lifelong posture of gratitude.

This is the GraceLife, and we are called to live it well. I hope and pray that you find yourself moving closer to this way of life with your church family. Because if Christ really dwells within us, the GraceLife will happen. And when it does, it attracts other people. In fact, they won't be able to stay away.

My exhortation to you is that you take each of the lessons that Philippians has for us and apply it in your life, and by doing so, draw closer to God and to God's children.

As Paul ended his letter, I end this book by borrowing his words from Philippians 4:23 (NIV):

The grace of the Lord Jesus Christ be with your spirit. Amen.

REFERENCES

Notes

1. "Introduction to Philippians." *ESV Study Bible.* Crossway, 2008, p. 2,275.

2. "The Epistle of Paul to the Philippians." In John MacArthur, *The MacArthur Bible Commentary: Unleashing God's Truth, One Verse at a Time,* Thomas Nelson, 2005, p. 1708–1709.

3. "Relentless." *Merriam-Webster.* https://www.merriam-webster.com/dictionary/relentless.

4. Malina, Bruce. *Timothy: Paul's Closest Associate.* Liturgical Press, 2008.

5. Yancey, Phillip. *What's So Amazing About Grace?* Zondervan, 1997.

6. Strong, James. "Para." *Strong's Exhaustive Concordance of the Bible.* Hunt & Eaton, New York, 1894.

7. Strong, James. "Kalo." *Strong's Exhaustive Concordance of the Bible*. Hunt & Eaton, New York, 1894.

8. Strong, James. "Parakalo." *Strong's Exhaustive Concordance of the Bible*. Hunt & Eaton, New York, 1894.

9. "Strong's G2169 – Eucharistia." *Blue Letter Bible*. https://www.blueletterbible.org/lang/lexicon/lexicon.cfm?t=ESV&strongs=g2169.

10. "Eu-." *Dictionary.com Unabridged*. Based on *Random House Unabridged Dictionary*, Random House, 2018. Quoted in *Dictionary.com*. https://www.dictionary.com/browse/eu-.

11. "Strong's G5485 – Charis." *Blue Letter Bible*. https://www.blueletterbible.org/lang/lexicon/lexicon.cfm?Strongs=G5485&t=ESV.

About the Author

Joe is the founding pastor of GraceLife Church (www.gracelifesrq.com) in Sarasota, FL. He holds a bachelor's degree in Biblical Studies and another in Pastoral Studies, as well as a master's degree in Theology.

After beginning vocational ministry at age eighteen, Joe spent his first twenty-two years of ministry as a youth pastor and outreach pastor in three different churches. He coached high school football and basketball for nearly twenty years.

In 2008, Joe founded Mobilepreacher.org (www.mobilepreacher.org), an organization designed to help seasoned ministers create ministries that might not fit inside traditional church walls. He is also the founder and executive director of the Nightlife Center in Sarasota (www.nightlifecenter.org).

Joe is husband to Laura and father to Ben. You can find him on Twitter (@mobilepreacher) and on Facebook (facebook.com/Mobilepreacher).

52194691R00083

Made in the USA
Columbia, SC
27 February 2019